e-Learning
2.0

Proven Practices and Emerging Technologies to Achieve Results

Anita Rosen

AMACOM

American Management Association
New York • Atlanta • Brussels • Chicago • Mexico City • San Francisco
Shanghai • Tokyo • Toronto • Washington, D.C.

Special discounts on bulk quantities of AMACOM books are
available to corporations, professional associations, and other
organizations. For details, contact Special Sales Department,
AMACOM, a division of American Management Association,
1601 Broadway, New York, NY 10019.
Tel.: 212-903-8316.   Fax: 212-903-8083.
Web site: www.amacombooks.org

This publication is designed to provide accurate and authoritative
information in regard to the subject matter covered. It is sold with the
understanding that the publisher is not engaged in rendering legal,
accounting, or other professional service. If legal advice or other expert
assistance is required, the services of a competent professional person
should be sought.

Library of Congress Cataloging-in-Publication Data

Rosen, Anita.
    E-learning 2.0 : proven practices and emerging technologies to achieve results / Anita Rosen.
        p.   cm.
    Includes bibliographical references and index.
    ISBN-13: 978-0-8144-1073-8
    ISBN-10: 0-8144-1073-1
    1. Employees—Training of—Data processing.   2. Employees—Training of—
Computer-assisted instruction.   3. Organizational learning.   4. Internet in education.
    I. Title.

HF5549.5.T7R599 2009
658.3'12402854678—dc22

                                                                    2008025589

Printing number

10   9   8   7   6   5   4   3   2   1

This book is dedicated to Al Moser.

A wonderful husband and

limitlessly knowledgeable technologist;

I thank Al for all his support and the time

he spent assuring that I understand

the implications of technologies

discussed in this book.

Contents

The Business Calculations and Business Objectives of e-Learning

For more than a decade, e-learning has been touted as the next big thing in training. Yet most organizations are still trying to figure out how to make it work. Perhaps part of the problem is that e-learning is a type of training or learning in which instructors and students interact at different times and in different spaces, with technology bridging the time-space gap and allowing learners to access training at their own pace and with methods that are convenient for them. A lot of companies have spent a lot of money creating a lot of projects—but they have not gotten what they thought they would get out of their investment in this still new technology.

Meanwhile, corporate training organizations are looking for better returns than they are currently receiving from their e-learning investment. While department-level personnel wait for executives to provide vision and goals, executives want trainers to develop a business plan to move training into the twenty-first century. Along the way, corporations spend billions of dollars on solutions selected on an ambiguous direction that is provided primarily by product vendors. Specifically, corporations

1

decide on an initiative to move to a new technology or methodology without understanding its implications for workers or without being able to measure the effectiveness of its implementation. When employees choose solutions, they tend to solve only their short-term needs—like, "How do I get this deliverable off of my desk?" What organizations need are clear visions, focused goals, and a better way to measure their learning objectives.

 By the end of this chapter, you should be able to:

- Understand the goal of training.
- Review sample ROI calculations.
- Understand how to measure and evaluate training.
- Identify your audience.
- Understand the biggest mistakes in top-down commands and bottom-up implementations.
- Understand communication within an organization.
- Learn how to get buy-in from trainers, employees, and SMEs.
- Understand where e-learning fits in.

1.1 The Goal of Training

This book takes a realistic and pragmatic look at e-learning. Over the last ten years, having worked with hundreds of organizations that are incorporating e-learning into their business practices, I have found that most training organizations have failed to achieve the expected returns on investment. I have seen department-level personnel waiting for their executives to provide vision and goals, while their executives, who have no practical experience with training, expect the trainers to develop a business plan to modernize the organization's training. This gap in expectations is fertile ground for vendors to dictate solutions, tactics, and strategies, which tend to benefit the product providers much more than their customers. Executive-level personnel go along with the vendor-provided solutions because they can present such solutions as "progress" to management, and contributor-level employees are happy just to get the tasks completed so that their managers stop asking about them. This cozy arrangement leaves employee training and productivity enhancement as an afterthought on the priority list. This book speaks to this current state of e-learning practices, identifying what is effective and what is counterproductive, and my theories and recommendations are illustrated by real-world case studies.

The irony of this commonplace approach to e-learning is that providing training over the Web, rather than as classroom training, creates more opportunities than people initially think. Many organizations initially look at moving training on-line to cut travel costs, to ease trainer schedules, or to provide training where it has not been available in the past. However, Web-based training is based on a different model than classroom training. A real benefit of moving training to an intranet/Internet-delivered model is that it provides an organization with availability and repetition.

- The always-on *availability* of the intranet/Internet subtly changes training. What was once a one-time training event can now be a corporate resource. Once implemented, e-learning provides homogeneous training, which is the same training, on the same day, for all employees.

- From a learning retention point-of-view, an on-line training event does not need to achieve as high a level of knowledge retention as classroom training because e-learning can be accessed at any time as a just-in-time resource. An effective e-learning model supports just-in-time training so that employees can refresh their memory when they need to carry out a procedure or when they run into an unexpected situation. With e-learning, employees can search a key word and access a course unit instead of simply having to remember each unit's content from top to bottom. In effect, employees learn how to find and access the information they need. Before the Internet, with its inherently easy access to corporate repositories of information, employees found that the hard

part of performing their jobs was finding where the procedures were spelled out. The benefit of using e-courses over
other methods of providing information, such as wikis or
on-line Word or PowerPoint documents, is that e-learning,
when developed properly, explains concepts and presents
the same information multiple ways, making it easier for
employees to understand new information or to follow new
procedures.

E-learning also enables organizations to tailor their training to meet
their specific goals. In a manufacturing organization, for example,
the goal is to ensure that each employee is efficient at the handful
of tasks he or she performs. In a service organization, the goal is to
increase productivity by ensuring that employees are knowledgeable about organizational offerings and that they provide a consistent experience. Managers undergo training to be able to properly
handle relationships and manage unexpected situations within the
confines of the organization's culture. Training and, by extension,
e-learning provide management with a tool to create a more flexible workforce. Employees can be trained to become intelligent
workers who know where to find information rather than to simply memorize procedures.

Of course, all these benefits cost money, but the return on investment is there if you know how to calculate it.

1.2 A Simple Example of Return-on-Investment (ROI) Calculations

E-learning is relatively new to most organizations. With any new
technology, service, or change in business practices, management
wants to quantify the cost and savings. Most organizations look at
return on investment (ROI) as the first step in justifying the cost of
a new service.

The ROI calculation for e-learning tends to be very simple. In
most situations an e-learning course replaces classroom training or
training workbooks. The ROI calculation identifies the current

cost to create and roll out a classroom course and compares it with the cost of creating an e-learning course and purchasing e-learning infrastructure.

For example, the Division of Development and Training in the Bureau of Human Resources is the organization in the Commonwealth of Pennsylvania Department of Labor and Industry that is responsible for managing compliance training and benefits for all 6,000 agency employees. Employees must receive training on a variety of mandated topics, including the State Employees Assistance Program, HIV/AIDS, bomb threats, and the like. Originally, all of this training was classroom based, delivered throughout the state for agency employees at various county, regional, and other local facilities. With tight travel budgets, the Commonwealth of Pennsylvania was looking for alternative ways to deliver training.

The Development and Training Division believed that migrating some of their courses to e-learning would lower training costs while providing agency employees with effective just-in-time training. They looked at their records and identified that, on average, the cost to roll out one training course was $85,000. This total took into account all the costs for travel, room, material, and food for both trainers and students. Having decided that not all courses were going to go on-line, they figured out how many courses they would convert to e-learning. For example, if they rolled out five classroom courses in a year, the real cost would be $425,000. If these courses were moved to an e-learning infrastructure, the cost would be about $200,000 for the year. Their savings for the year would be $425,000 − $200,000 = $225,000); their return on investment would be $225,000 ÷ $200,000 = 1.125, or 11.25%.

However, cost varies. Some organizations find that they need large, centralized databases to handle their training needs, whereas other organizations find that simpler solutions meet their needs. The Commonwealth of Pennsylvania went with a simple solution: With ReadyGo WCB and ReadyGo SST, for an outlay of $2,500, they saved their department over $400,000 in training costs.

1.3 How to Measure and Evaluate Training

Return on Investment

Return on investment is easy to calculate when effectiveness is easy to measure. Yet, although managers move into e-learning presumably understanding its benefit, they often run into problems in measuring, managing, and understanding whether the new initiative is working.

Setting the Goals to Reap the Rewards

E-learning is no different from any other initiative. When consulting with businesses about new technology initiatives, I frequently have to take managers back to the basics. With every successful project, the same basic question needs to be asked: What is the goal? This exercise is necessary at a global level for the infrastructure conversation, as well as at a course or course series level. The people responsible for executing the project have to stay focused on the goal. The process is the same regardless of where the execution takes place; the initiative has to meet its organizational goals.

The five questions that must be answered both globally and at the course level are:

1. Why are you doing this in the first place?
2. What is this infrastructure and course supposed to do?
3. Do you have an effective plan?
4. Have you created metrics for success?
5. How will you identify whether the project is a success?

Most organizations can easily answer the first two questions; they know why they're training and what they need to accomplish. Where corporate measurement starts falling apart is with the last three questions. In particular, rarely do organizations have clear answers for questions four and five.

Many times, the reason for failed projects goes back to a lack of concrete business objectives up front. Achieving success in a project is difficult when you don't clearly know how you are going to measure success. When asked to provide their e-learning goals, managers usually come up with answers like, "Put e-learning infrastructure in place," "Put my PowerPoint presentations online," "Create a course," "Use Flash/Dreamweaver/PowerPoint," "Improve sales, "Reduce costs," "Train employees," and "Save money." [Instructional designers (IDs) might respond with, "Create a course with instructional design."]

None of these statements really means anything. They are not true goals. They do not answer the basic questions: "Why do you want to do it? What do you think you will get out of it?" For an initiative to be successful, someone has to create goals that are measurable, actionable, and realistic. The goals need to mean something so that solutions can be targeted. Examples of such goals are:

- Have a mechanism to track 80 percent of our employee training completion status by the fourth quarter.
- Move 50 percent of all training courses to the Internet within eight quarters.
- Have 90 percent of our employees certified by June 30.
- Increase awareness of our products by 25 percent for 100 percent of our employees in sales and marketing by the end of the second quarter.
- Have a 20 percent increase in knowledge of our new services among our branch staff by the end of this quarter.

Creating measurable and actionable goals sounds like a small task, but it makes a difference. By writing down and quantifying the goals, employees responsible for execution have something that they can shoot for and management has something that they can measure.

A meaningful goal has two characteristics: a number and a due date.

1. For a goal to be measurable, it should contain a *number*, such as, "track 80 percent," "move 50 percent," "90 percent certification," "increase awareness by 25 percent," or "increase knowledge by 20 percent." Typically, measurement is a two-step process. You first need a benchmark number, such as current costs, the number of employees trained last year, or the current level of product awareness. If you don't know the current status, you need to find out. The baseline may be realized by looking at past records or by conducting an online survey or online pretest. Without a baseline number, any other number is meaningless. With a baseline, you can implement a project and identify its success. If it is impossible or difficult to quantify the number up front, make sure this is stipulated in your goal, or choose another goal.

2. To be achievable, a goal is must have a *due date*. Without a deadline, the goal has no focus. Once goals are created, they can be used to keep the e-learning project focused, get funding, prove the value to the company, and get other departments to buy into the process.

When creating goals, start the process by writing down what you want to achieve. Then prioritize and refine these goals. For example, in moving their state compliance courses online, an organization identified the following goals:

1. All eight state compliance courses are to be available online by January 30.

2. One hundred percent of employees must be able to access and complete the courses by June 30.

3. One hundred percent of employees must be able to receive a grade of 80 percent or better on the final test.

Next, put the goals through an evaluative process:

- *Prioritize your goals.* Of the goals in the preceding list, for example, is it more important that everyone has access or that a grade point average is achieved? Do all the courses need to be available on the same day?

- *Review your goals for achievability.* Some goals are easy to achieve, others more difficult. Difficulty can arise from the time allotted, the technology available, the skills of employees, the cost of implementation, or just internal politics. Identify which goals are hard, medium, or easy to achieve and create achievable goals. For example, some goals might take a long time to accomplish. If you identify a hard-to-reach goal, mitigate the uncertainty by creating milestones on the way to the main goal. For example, you might change the first goal to read, "The first four corporate compliance courses must be available online by January 30." Then add a new goal: "The second four corporate compliance courses will be available online by March 30." (By the way, although course designers like to include instructional design in their course goals, other departments typically do not understand or care about instructional design. Instructional design is not a goal; it is what a course designer uses to achieve the goal. For example, how do you achieve a company-wide 80 percent GPA for the goal? Answer: You create a course with instructional design.)

- *Align your e-learning goals with existing organizational goals.* Identify the managers whose employees are going to take the training, and determine on what basis are they being measured? If the course is for a new product and a sales manager has quota targets for the product, create training goals that align with the manager's needs. The closer your training goals mesh with corporate and management goals, the more buy-in your initiative will have from other departments.

1.4 Identifying Your Audience

Many organizations stop after identifying their goals and then don't understand why their initiative doesn't meet expectations. The next step in meeting goals is to identify the audience and to make sure that your initiative can realistically meet your audience's needs. Goals that are not attuned to your audience's expectations will not succeed. Toward this end, before creating any e-learning initiative, you need to:

1. Clearly identify your audience by creating a learner demographic profile.
2. Identify the experience you want your learners to have.

Identify Learning Demographics

Make sure you know who will be taking the course. A broad audience definition may include prospects, customers, employees, vendors, or business partners. Before purchasing infrastructure or creating a course, however, you need to answer this list of questions:

- What group or groups are you trying to reach?
- Who will take the course?
- Who else will take the course?
- What new audiences might you reach?
- What does the learner look like demographically?
- Why are the learners taking the course?
- What do they want to achieve?

Based on whom you are reaching, you need to create a demographic overview for each learner. The types of questions you need to pose are:

- What type of job function do they have: sales, technical, finance?
- What language(s) do they speak, and is their primary language English?

- What country do they live in—the United States or a country where they are accessing the course over a slow connection or a smartphone?
- How educated are they—high school, college, advanced degree?
- How technical are they—are they doctors or patients?
- How old are they—teenagers? If the class is for senior citizens, do you need to consider font size and audio requirements?

The information you gather by asking these questions may make you refocus or even change your course so that it reaches your intended market. A customer course explaining a new service that is focused on high school students may be very different from one intended for retirees.

Most importantly, you need to understand the learners' environment:

- Are learners accessing the course:
  - From the office?
  - At home?
  - While traveling?
  - All of the above?
- How fast is the slowest learner's Internet access? Does your course perform over the learner's lines?
- What browsers are they using—and which versions of Microsoft IE, Mozilla, Safari, Netscape? Does your course support learners' browsers?
- What size(s) monitor do they have? Does your course scale to fit?
- What resolution monitor do they have? Can they view the course easily, or do they need to scroll?
- Can they use audio? Are they in a cube? Do they have headphones? Does their information technology (IT) department let audio stream over their network?

- Do any learners have an impairment, such as:
  - Color blindness? (20 percent of men are color blind.)
  - Blindness?
  - Hearing impairment?

If you are in an environment that is not tightly controlled by IT, you most likely don't know the answers to most of these questions. However, not knowing the answers is an answer. In that case, you need to build your course for the lowest common denominator, that is, for the individuals who, for example, have unique mobility or accessibility issues, who have the least sophisticated technology, or who have learning impairments that may limit how they can learn. Your goal is to ensure that your courses are accessible to the widest possible audience: You never want learners to say that they could not take the training course because it did not work on their computer or because it was beyond their individual ability.

Identify the Learner Experience

Without a clear idea of your audience and the experience you want them to have, you will purchase the wrong infrastructure and create unacceptable courses. The remainder of the book deals with the learning experience, offering many examples to help you determine what experiences are important to your organization.

1.5 Biggest Mistakes in Top-Down "Command" (CS) and Bottom-Up Implementations

Whereas training infrastructure tends to result from a top-down initiative, course development tends to be a bottom-up implementation. Each approach can have its strengths and weaknesses. Top-down and bottom-up mistakes both have one thing in common: The people choosing the solution focus on their needs, not the learners' experience or the organizations goals. Top-down mistakes usually consist of installing a learning management system

(LMS) or learning content management system (LCMS) that doesn't meet the organizations needs; bottom-up mistakes tend to involve using processes and tools that are easy for the trainer but that create a subpar experience for the learner.

Top-Down Mistakes

Organizations need to decide on their goals and identify the infrastructure they need to achieve their goals. A *learning management systems (LMS)* is a database application that creates a self-serve learning environment: laying out what courses need to be taken and which courses have been taken, serving courses, and storing employee training information including testing and status results. A *learning content management system (LCMS)* is an LMS on steroids. In addition to having LMS features, an LCMS integrates course creation with course management. Not all organizations need to purchase an LMS or LCMS to create a corporate online university or to serve employees courses. Some organizations are fine with a *test engine*, which registers students and saves student information. It does not include the front-end student status information found in an LMS or an LCMS.

One common top-down mistake is that management tends to jumps to big solutions and to justify the solutions by using an ROI before they clearly identify their goals and audience. Specifically, the learner experience and the course creator experience need to be identified before a solution is chosen. These steps are difficult for organizations that have yet to create any of their own e-learning courses. For organizations that have already developed and used e-learning, they to be easier because both the learners and the course creator can be polled to identify what is working and what is not and to identify what features are needed to create a better experience. Whether the initiative is new or not, don't get into too detail at this point. No existing system will meet all of your organization's individual needs. Just identify an overall experience and make sure your solution can respond.

. . . .

Case Study:
Texas Department of Transportation

The Texas Department of Transportation (TxDOT), in cooperation with local and regional officials, is responsible for planning, designing, building, operating, and maintaining the state of Texas's transportation system. TxDOT has almost 15,000 employees who need to be trained on the department's policies and procedures. The TxDOT training department thought that e-learning would be a relatively easy, cost-effective, and productive way for them to roll out many of their training courses. For the training department to get an e-learning initiative approved, they felt that they needed to provide more then an ROI; they needed to show that e-learning worked for them. They purchased canned courses that came with an embedded LMS. They then augmented this purchase with an e-learning authoring tool and a collection engine so that they could turn a couple of their standard classroom courses into e-learning courses. They served these e-learning courses to a pilot group of employees who were required to take the training. Janet Risovi, the TxDOT trainer, was happy to report that learner feedback from these e-learning courses was better then expected. People appreciated having the option of taking the courses on-line. The ROI/cost saving was immediate and impressive. This trial gave the training department the ability to present real savings and a proven solution.

The state approved an initiative to fund training on the Web. The Tx-DOT wanted one solution that could serve canned courses, along with internal courses and simulations, and that connected to their People-Soft system, which was used to manage their employee training curriculum. Since the training department had already created and served e-learning, they understood the desired features. They found an LMS that met the department's needs; it could serve their canned courses and courses built in-house. They branded their e-learning portal iWay, which serves all 350 available courses, updates People-Soft, and provides the reports the agency needs. This bottom-up initiative meets the needs of the learners and solves many existing training needs the organization has struggled with.

● ● ● ● ● ● ● ● ● ● ●

Another mistake when implementing top-down initiatives is not thinking through the information that your organization wants to save and identifying the reports that it must have. If you purchase a system that saves little or no information, you have lost all learner data forever. Disk space is cheap. Identify the maximum information you might ever need, and make sure your solution can save and store it. Don't forget reports. Make sure your system includes reports and, more importantly, has an easy way for you to get to your data so that you can create your own reports.

Some top-down initiatives try to solve too many problems with one solution. Many LMS and LCMS vendors tout their ability to solve all content management problems. This is a compelling argument because IT organizations would rather support fewer systems than more. Focus on the issues you want to solve, and buy the product that solves those issues. Managing more applications might seem hard, but having one solution that fails to adequately solve any issue doesn't move the business ahead. For example, if your goal is to have all your PowerPoint presentations available to all employees, buy a content management solution. If your goal is to serve courses and save test scores, buy a test engine. If you are trying to create a learning portal, buy an LMS.

However, don't overbuy. Salespeople love to tout obscure features. Focus on features that are important to your organization and buy them. If you use Web-based tools to create your courses, you do not put limits on the learning environment, and your courses can be served by an LMS and accessed by a content management solution.

Bottom-Up Mistakes

One bottom-up mistake is that many such initiatives view e-learning not as a different approach to training, but rather as a different delivery mechanism. Specifically trainers choose solutions that are as close as possible to what they are currently doing without taking in account what they could be or should be doing to create a positive on-line learning experience. Management, for its part, often does not know how to assess a good e-learning course from a poor one. All they know how to do is look at ROI, but a good e-learning course does not save the company any more money than a poor e-learning one.

In fact, good e-learning may cost more because it takes the trainer longer to produce. From a goal and objective point a view, a good course should reap more benefits then a poor one. For example, a trainer records the audio of a classroom session, includes it with a PowerPoint presentation for Web delivery, and calls the package e-learning.

- From the trainer's point of view, this is just an easy way to get the e-learning initiative off the desk.
- From the learner's point of view, the resulting voice-annotated slide show is boring.
- From the corporate point of view, employees are spending time taking a course that is not maximizing what could be achieved.

This last point is probably the most costly to the organization—and needlessly. If 1,000 employees need to take a one-hour course, the course represents 1,000 man-hours. If it takes a course creator 5 hours to create a poor course and 40 hours to create an excellent one, the course creator might be viewed as having wasted 35 hours. However, if 1,000 man-hours can be spent in a productive session instead of a fruitless one, that is a tremendously valuable use of time.

Typically, course quality tends to be in direct proportion to the understanding that the organization has of what a good and effective course looks like. Yet often, the organization does not know what an effective course looks like. Many learners have never experienced a good e-learning course; they give thumbs up to a bad e-learning course because they would rather spend five hours at their desk or in their home office then a day in a classroom. If you are uncertain about how to identify a poor course from a good one, this book gives you tips, techniques, and best-use practices for creating effective e-learning. Course creators can use these ideas to create better courses, and management can use them to identify effective strategies for managing and focusing courses and thus to achieve higher productivity.

1.6 Communications Within an Organization

A fundamental issue when implementing any new initiative is corporate communication. Do the people at the top communicate what they want to see accomplished to the people executing the solution? Is the communication couched in terms the receivers understand? Do the people executing the solution communicate to management what they are doing in terms that management understands? For any initiative to work effectively, all tiers of the organization need to communicate with each other. The central focal point in effectively communicating at any level of the organization is the initiative's goals.

Part of the implementation, therefore, is to talk the right talk. Trainers are focused on creating training and many times get caught up in the how-to of creating training. Trainers focus on the task at hand, talking about effective instructional design.

Management, on the other hand, tends to push initiatives down the corporate ladder. They may say, "We are implementing e-learning to cut travel costs by 50 percent." However, they do not define what other benefits they want to reap. Or they might say, "Put all our PowerPoint presentations on-line so that everyone has access." But they don't provide guidelines on how the PowerPoint presentations are to be used. Without specifics, such as realistic, measurable, and actionable goals, employees tend to find the easiest solution to get the task off their desks.

Without effective communication, the synergies that are possible between the top-down and the bottom-up initiatives misfire. (Sometimes, even with proper communication many mistakes are made.) To effectively reap the benefits of new initiatives, all levels of the organization need to communicate using a shared vocabulary. Goal setting and audience identification can be used as the basis of this communication. The results of these sessions need to be agreed upon and shared throughout the organization.

To speak to management, trainers need to use management terminology. They need to state the course's goals. If there is a problem with the course flow or structure, they need to speak in terms of its effect on reaching the goals. Trainers who do not use goals as the centerpiece for their conversation with management may find themselves talking about the how-to side of the issue—instructional design—and find that management just isn't listening.

From the management point of view, instructional design is nothing more than what course creators use to achieve management's goals. Course creators therefore need to focus on the benefits of instructional design. For example, "Our goal for this training initiative is to increase employee productivity by 30 percent. To achieve this goal we need to ensure that the training course meets our requirements. We need more time to better structure the material so that employees will reap the full productivity benefits."

1.7 Getting Buy-In from Trainers, Employees, and Subject Matter Experts

Getting buy-in from trainers, employees, and subject matter experts (SMEs) is always an issue when creating an e-learning initiative. Top-down initiatives tend to get better buy-in because management has the power to ensure compliance, or they can put pressure on underlings to support their pet initiatives. Getting employees to buy in on the training is easy when it is organizationally mandated or when employees are required to take the course for some form of certification.

Getting employees to take courses that help them perform their jobs better is a lot harder. To get people interested, optional courses need to be compelling and relevant. Throughout this book we discuss strategies you can use to make your courses more compelling.

Although you're on your own to create relevant courses, a tip is to look to organizational goals to see what is considered relevant.

Buy-in is particularly difficult in bottom-up initiatives when a peer is attempting to solicit other trainers to develop e-learning or to get an SME to help create a course. Most commonly, trainers and SMEs are busy performing their jobs, and e-learning is just a distraction. Trainers and SMEs use every excuse in the book to avoid working on an e-learning course. The usual root causes of this resistance are that trainers and SMEs do not buy in to the benefits of the project and that it sounds like a lot of work to create e-learning. They have never created e-learning, and they don't know how big a project it will be, how long it will take, how steep the learning curve will be, and whether the end result will have any relevance.

To get trainers and SMEs to support an e-learning initiative takes work up front. Those who are trying to get buy-in need to create goals that are aligned with the trainer's or SME's goals. They then need to present a simple plan that highlights the steps for the trainer or SME to take to turn what they have into e-learning. Most importantly, they need to provide options and information that are simple and straightforward for the trainer or SME.

· · · · · · · · · · · ·

Case Study:
National Semiconductor Corporation

National Semiconductor (National) is a manufacturing company with over 8,500 employees. In their central training group, called National Semiconductor University (NSU), two people are dedicated to e-learning. The total training department includes an additional 20 people located throughout the world. The centralized training group is too small to handle all the course creation capabilities that SMEs request. To handle the overwhelming course needs, they decided to create a process whereby SMEs create the training and the centralized training people support their effort.

Figure 1.1 National Semiconductor SME project flow.

National Semiconductor University Web Course Development Process

Phase		Deliverable	Gating Activity
Assess Diagnose the learning need; summarize and communicate the purpose of the planned course		Requirements Summary	• Review with NSU • Go/NoGo decision
Design Create a framework for an effective e-learning experience		Design Document	• Review with NSU • If decision is made to move forward, NSU provides SME with ReadyGo software • Define/agree on development timeline and check-ins with NSU
Develop Build a high-quality course		Review version of complete course	• Check in with NSU as needed during development –monthly at minimum • When review version of course is ready, meet with NSU for initial review • Identify/complete edits before alpha release
Test Assure that course gets thorough review by experts and sample learners		Launch-ready version of course	• Coordinate alpha and beta reviews with NSU
Launch Assure that course availability and registration/participation procedures are properly communicated to target audience		E-Learning Launch Document Effective course launch	• Coordinate with NSU
Evaluate & Maintain Keep content updated and responsive to user feedback		Post-launch evaluation Maintenance and update plan	• Coordinate with NSU

Initially, NSU personnel created a six-step process to help SMEs develop e-learning courses. (See Figure 1.1.) Parts of the process had SMEs use fill-in-the-blank deliverables and take an e-learning course explaining how to create effective on-line courses. With each step of the process, an NSU consultant met with the SME. The NSU consultant assisted the SME, reviewed the goals and objective development with the SME, and made a go/no-go decision.

1. The first step was assessment of the learning need and of the purpose of the training.
2. During the second step, the SME was trained in the basics of creating a good course and given an authoring tool to create the course.
3. As the third step, the SME built the course. During this step the NSU representative was available to support the SME and to ensure quality.

4. Step four was quality assurance.

5. In step five the course was launched.

6. The sixth and last step of the process was the course evaluation, in which changes or updates were made.

Stephen Hellie, Technical e-learning Training Manager for NSU, says he found that the original process provided an effective flow but the forms and required approval steps became a barrier for most SMEs. Having modified the process slightly, he found that SMEs delivered better information and less resistance when a combination of interviews and informal conversations were conducted, instead of having the SME fill out forms.

NSU also decided not to give an e-learning authoring tool to SMEs who were creating only one or two courses. Only SMEs who are creating a series of courses are trained on how to use the tool. This minimizes resistance to learning a new software tool and makes the process more productive.

What works well for SMEs is to let them create the e-learning course in the tool they are most comfortable using, usually Word or Power-Point. The NSU staff then works directly with the SME using the existing material, reviewing it and helping to move it to the next level.

Although most SMEs have never been exposed to instructional design theories, Stephen has found that SMEs are open to coaching and to his suggestions because he simplifies their workload. They see the benefits of delivering information in a clearer, easier to understand, more digestible format.

Once the NSU staff member and the SME feel comfortable with the course material, the staff member uses the e-learning authoring tool to put the course in an on-line format and posts it to a preproduction server for the SME to review. The SME now has an opportunity to view the material as a Web course and to work with the NSU staff member to make changes.

Stephen and his coworkers view themselves as consultants. They find that SMEs are hungry for help and appreciate how easy NSU has made it for them to turn their material into e-learning courses. The positive experience pays off: Word of mouth is a wonderful advertisement. SMEs at National are very open to creating e-learning. Stephen says he rarely has to chase down SMEs to get them to work with him.

• • • • • • • • • • •

1.8 Where e-Learning Fits In

E-learning is not a one-size-fits-all solution for every problem, and it will never replace classroom training. E-learning is a great solution for some training needs. Many organizations have found that e-learning can effectively be used to move many classroom training sessions on-line. For courses that need role-playing or hands-on access to materials, e-learning can be used to augment the training, thus saving time and allowing more people to be trained.

• • • • • • • • • • •

Case Study:
Hospital Liaison Committee of Jehovah's
Witnesses in Leicester, United Kingdom

Laurence Wilson, principle of Virtual Pedagogue, an e-learning training company, is also the chairman of the Hospital Liaison Committee of Jehovah's Witnesses in Leicester, United Kingdom. Because the Jehovah's Witnesses' faith forbids the acceptance of donor blood transfusions, Laurence was especially interested to promote information concerning transfusion alternatives. Laurence took responsibility for devising the pilot training course so that medical staff at five hospitals in the Trent and Leicester area of the United Kingdom could learn about an alternative to donor blood transfusion called intraoperative cell salvage (ICS).

With increasing restrictions imposed on volunteer blood donors in the interest of blood safety and with the public more aware than ever of issues in receiving a blood transfusion, clinicians and patients are interested in exploring viable alternatives to conventional allogeneic (donor) blood transfusions. Intraoperative cell salvage (ICS) recycles a patient's own blood for use during operations, avoiding the need for a transfusion. The goal of this program is to raise awareness of ICS, roll out training, and ultimately create a best practice blueprint to train potentially thousands of hospital staff within the United Kingdom's National Health Service (NHS).

The challenge is how to train large numbers of health care staff without pulling them off the floor or compromising operating room schedules. E-learning turned out to be an excellent solution. Wilson explained:

> I know how to move classroom training to the web. I worked with hospital anesthesiologists to develop a series of courses that medical staff can take when their schedule allows. We used these online courses to prepare medical staff for a classroom session where they receive practical experience; they then practiced on a dummy in a simulation center; finally they had supervised, hands on session in the operating room before receiving a certificate. . . . A blended learning approach really saved time, cut costs, and allowed us to train more medical staff. The UK National Training Awards organization was very impressed with our effective e-learning course design and our ability to understand where and when to use e-learning and classroom training.

After the successful pilot, the United Kingdom's National Blood Service (NBS) rolled the program out across the country.

• • • • • • • • • • •

1.9 Checklist

___ Five questions must be answered, both globally and at the course level:

1. Why are you doing this in the first place?
2. What is this infrastructure or course supposed to do?
3. Do you have an effective plan?
4. Have you created metrics for success?
5. How will you identify whether the project is a success?

__ Create a set of measurable and actionable goals.

__ Identify your audience.

__ Before creating any e-learning initiative, you need to:

   1. Clearly identify your audience by creating a learner demographic profile.
   2. Identify the experience you want your learner to have.

__ Before purchasing infrastructure or creating a course, you need to answer this list of questions:

   1. What group or groups are you trying to reach?
   2. Who will take the course?
   3. Who else will take the course?
   4. What new audiences might you reach?
   5. What does the learner look like (demographically)?
   6. Why are the learners taking the course?
   7. What do they want to achieve?

__ Based on whom you are reaching, you need to create a demographic overview for each learner. The types of questions you need to understand are:

   1. What type of job function do they have: sales, technical, finance?
   2. What language(s) do they speak, and is their primary language English?
   3. What country do they live in—the United States or a country where they are accessing the course over a slow connection or a smartphone?
   4. How educated are they:—high school, college, advanced degree?
   5. How technical are they—are they doctors or patients?
   6. How old are they—teenagers? If the class is for senior citizens, do you need to consider font size and audio requirements?

__ Most importantly, you need to understand the environment that the learner is using. You need to know:

1. Are learners accessing the course:

   - From the office?
   - At home?
   - While traveling?
   - All of the above?

2. How fast is the slowest learner's Internet access? Does your course perform over the learner's lines?
3. What browsers are they using—and which versions of Microsoft IE, Mozilla, Safari, Netscape? Does your course support learners' browsers?
4. What size(s) monitor do they have? Does your course scale to fit?
5. What resolution monitor do they have? Can they view the course easily, or do they need to scroll?
6. Can they use audio? Are they in a cube? Do they have headphones? Does their information technology (IT) department let audio stream over their network?
7. Do any learners have an impairment, such as:

   - Color blindness? (20% of men are color blind.)
   - Blindness?
   - Hearing impairment?

CHAPTER

2.0

e-Learning Strategies

After identifying your e-learning goals and audience, it is important to identify where your organization is in the acceptance process of e-learning and to develop a roadmap identifying the strategies you will employ to get where you want to go. Before developing a roadmap, you need to identify the terrain of this new initiative. This chapter provides insights into how to identify where you are in the process and the basics of e-learning development so that you can identify your e-learning terrain.

 By the end of this chapter, you should be able to:

- Understand the five stages of adopting new technologies.
- Outline the five developmental stages of Web sites.
- List the five developmental stages of Web courses.
- Explain the fundamentals of creating on the Web.
- Describe the characteristics of good e-learning.
- Discuss the current state of Web courses.

2.1 Five Stages of Adopting New Technologies

Over the past 25 years, the technology sector has seen many new trends and technologies move from rough concept to delivered products and then to new business approaches. In all cases, organizations go through five stages when assimilating the new trends and technologies into the way they do business (see Figure 2.1):

1. Denial

2. Outsourcing

3. PowerPoint

4. Execution

5. Integration

As with everything, some organizations spend a lot of time in one stage, while others transition quickly to the next stage. How quickly organizations go through the different stages is usually tied to how focused management is on actualizing the technology. For many organizations it takes years to synthesize and adapt to new ways of doing business. Depending on the trend or technology,

Figure 2.1 Market adoption: As organizations adopt new technologies, the use of those technologies within the organization grows.

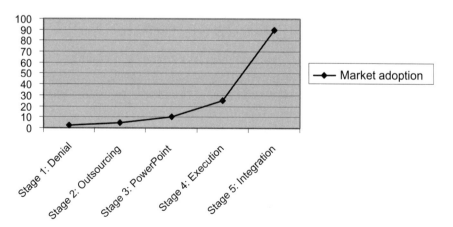

even individual employees and departments within an organization may be in different stages at the same time.

Stage 1: Denial

At first management and employees deny that they need to modify how they do business and adopt a new or emerging trend or technology. Fundamentally, most people do not want to try new things. Many people are inherently afraid of change and will do anything to maintain the status quo. Other people may be curious or interested in new technologies but feel overwhelmed, and they might fear the impact of change on their currently full plate. Very few people have the desire, skill, or acumen to be able to consider a new technology, figure out how it applies to them, and then present the new tend or technology within their organization to get it adopted. Most people try to marginalize an upcoming trend or technology so that they don't need to learn something new; they don't want anything new added to their already busy schedule.

So, during the denial stage, when a new trend or technology is presented, most people make comments like, "Sounds like the latest trend that someone is trying to sell to us," or "This doesn't rally apply to our business." Of course, this is true with some trends and technologies, but with other trends and technologies this is just a delaying tactic to put off dealing with the ramifications of a changing business model.

Stage 2: Outsourcing

At some point the technology or trend can no longer be ignored. The pressure to do something with the new trend or technology is felt, and it may come from external sources or from management. Sometimes the pressure is bottom-up. For example, in the 1980s information technology (IT) departments did not believe that personal computers (PCs) were their responsibility. They wanted to stick to centrally managed mainframes and did everything possible to outlaw PCs on the desktops. Eventually they were forced to embrace PCs when their organization was overwhelmed by all the PCs that user departments bought. More recently, organizations have needed to embrace and better manage cell phones and personal digital assistants (PDAs).

More typically, such pressure comes from vendors, consultants, trade groups, business groups, and magazines. These outside influencers constantly bombard organizations with information on the new trend or technology, compelling employees to at least say that they too exploring the possibilities. In this stage, businesspeople start questioning whether the technology applies to them, and the conversation usually starts with something like, "Yeah, we need to look into this." Employees start to realize that they need to take the trend seriously—to learn about it, figure out how it applies to their business, and take the risks to implement—even though they might not feel ready to do so. This ambivalence is not unusual. Most people fear having to climb a new learning curve, especially multidimensional ones. Employees need to learn about a new technology. Then they need to figure out how it applies to their business. Then they need to modify how they work to integrate it. That is a lot to embrace all at once. The reaction of most employees is to see how quickly they can get the new initiative off their desks entirely or make it someone else's responsibility.

Outsourcing tends to be the quickest and easiest solution for getting a trend or technology off your desk. The learning curve may be steep and long, the cost of equipment and materials may be significant, and the individual's skill set may not be suitable. To get over these hurdles, people commonly look for someone else to take over the initiative: They outsource.

The biggest downside to outsourcing is that no outsider understands your company, your product line, your services, or your culture better than you and your colleagues. When you outsource early, you tend to throw the project at a vendor. You don't really understand what you want, you are not ready to embrace the trend or technology, and you just want it off your desk. Obviously, outsourcing the adoption of a trend or technology at this stage results in limited success in the best of cases. If the primary goal for out-sourcing at this stage is to get the project off your desk, the goals and business objectives have not been thoroughly thought through. At this stage you are relying on an outside organization to clair-voyantly understand your corporate culture and business objectives and to successfully deliver a project that you don't yet understand.

Stage 3: PowerPoint

In this stage everyone is mentioning the development in their Pow-erPoint presentations on strategic and tactical planning that needs to be approved, funded, and executed. The initial mention of the technology is primarily for cosmetic reasons; that is, employees want to show that they haven't fallen behind, even though they still don't understand the impacts of the new systems.

At some point, however, the organization starts to adopt the new trend or technology. The understanding of its related issues moves from an abstraction to a tangible reality. Organizations begin to realize its relevance and importance. They identify that they need to integrate this new trend or technology into their daily business procedures. Perhaps the organization has gone through stage 2 with limited success. Perhaps it has outsourced the initiative, learning what works or. more importantly, what does not work. During the PowerPoint stage, the IT organization may be installing infrastructure technologies to support the new trend or technology, but internal execution of the project has not begun in earnest.

Stage 4: Execution

Eventually the organization begins to fully execute the plans iden-tified in the PowerPoint presentations. Employees have embraced the concept of the new trend or technology, and managers refer to it regularly in conversations—for example, "Did you Google this already?" Resources and budgets have been allocated. Responsi-bility and accountability for the success of the project have been as-signed. This stage demonstrates a level of organizational knowledge and awareness. The organization understands the importance and relevance of the new trend. A business plan that is relevant, with reasonable and obtainable goals, has been created, and people will be held accountable for its successful implementation. Goals and measurements are being put in place.

Stage 5: Integration

At some point the trend has been integrated within the organization, executed, and in use as intended. It no longer is a new way of doing business but an expected way of doing business. Just think about phones, faxes, PCs, instant messaging, and cell phones. Each of these technologies was once new: each went through a corporate adoption cycle. Now they are all standard business tools that have modified how business is conducted.

Let's apply this adoption cycle first to Web sites and then to e-learning.

2.2 Five Developmental Stages of Web Sites

Over the past 15 years, the Internet and its graphical user interface, the World Wide Web, have gone from being a simple way to send short messages to becoming a major communications, advertising, and fulfillment channel. Over the past 15 years, Web sites have gone through the same five stages that other new technologies have undergone: denial, outsourcing, Power Point, execution, and integration. These stages highlight how organizations undertake to accept, integrate, and internalize trends and technologies into the way they do business.

In this section, we look at the five developmental stages of Web sites over the years. By understanding the stages that Web sites have gone through, we can understand how Web courses and e-learning also have evolved—and we can understand the characteristics that make these technologies useful to organizations and their employees today.

Denial

In 1995 very few companies had a presence on the Internet. When Netscape went public, the press started buzzing about how the Internet was the future, yet very few companies rushed to create an Internet presence. Most did not see how this new technology was going to have an effect on how they did business.

Outsourcing

It quickly became evident that organizations needed to have a Web presence. Most companies did not have a clear idea what this presence should be or how the Internet would affect their business. They definitely did not believe that the internet would be a core business channel. Companies hired Web design firms and told them to create a Web site. Often management gave the Web designers company brochures and not much else. Because the brochures were created to be distributed on paper, the resulting on-line brochure Web sites were rather bleak. The content tended to be long and difficult to read on-line, the site was clumsy and difficult to navigate, and downloading site information took a long time because the graphics were developed for print pieces. These early Web sites were viewed not as an interactively changing business channel, but as a one-time event that was outsourced quickly so that employees could focus on what the company perceived to be the real business channels.

As Internet usage grew, most companies started to change and updated their Web sites. Upper management became aware of the benefit of a Web presence; they tended to include discussion of the Internet in their agenda. The next-generation sites were internally focused. There was a lot of information on investor relations, mission statements, job openings, press releases, and messages from the company's president. Topics that were more appropriate for an intranet (internal) Web site or for a limited section of a corporate Web site formed the core of the information provided. These second-generation Web sites were still graphically heavy. They were not focused on the customer or built to move business ahead. Companies were still outsourcing their Web sites, and graphic artists were still laying out and designing sites based on the principles of the print-based communication world. Features of these sites included:

- Click-through start pages (pages that provide no information, just pretty graphics that the visitor needs to click on to get to information).

- Large product pictures and more than one flashing or animated graphic per page that the visitor had to view before getting product information.

- Unsearchable sites that consisted of graphics, not text, because graphic artists, who like to precisely control physical layout, turned text into pictures.

The pages looked great but could not be read by any search engines, and no one focused the site on the customer's experience. Moving business ahead was apparently not a goal. No one inside the business was embracing the Web site as a fundamental business vehicle. No one saw it as a business application. Rather, it was viewed as little more than a one-time deliverable built to satisfy a demand from upper management.

PowerPoint

Eventually organizations caught on to the power of the Web, perhaps creating an e-business position staffed by a person with the authority and responsibility to integrate business activates into the Web site. From outside the company, Web sites still looked as they were driven by graphic artists, not business processes. Internally, the company was shifting how they viewed the Web.

In the late 1990s, I visited a company as an e-business consultant. The company's Web site had lots of pretty moving pictures but no real content or applications. When I mentioned to a vice president that the organization's Web site was not integrated into its business, she replied, "I have to disagree; the Web is completely integrated into the way we do business. Everyone's PowerPoint presentation has a Web site deliverable." However, all these PowerPoint presentations were not affecting the organization's Web site. Their web site was very primitive even though internally the organization understood the power of the Web. Management was laying plans to use the Web as a new business channel, but their Web site did not yet reflect this understanding.

Execution

The strategic and tactical planning presented in the PowerPoint stage needs to be funded and executed. Depending on the complexity of the project, this could take weeks to years before an application shows up on a Web site.

During execution, organizations may continue to outsource Web development. However, their attitude and level of control are different in the execution stage than they were in outsourcing stage. Instead of throwing brochures at a graphic artist and asking for a Web site, managers create goals and objectives. They became interactively involved in the process of creating the Web site or Web application. The Web presence moves away from being something to be avoided or minimized, becoming the central component of a project with a specific chain of responsibility.

Integration

Currently, for many organizations, the Web site is the central conduit for customers to conduct business with them. It is the first place people go to get the introductory information, and it can be a central channel for purchasing, delivery, support, and follow-up interactions. A Web site provides customers and prospects with real-time applications and information. Internally, applications developed for the Web site are not considered busy work, but rather a primary channel for distributing information to customers and prospects. At the integration stage, the Internet is completely integrated into how an organization conducts business.

2.3 Five Developmental Stages of Web Courses

The delivery of training through the Web is a relatively recent trend and technology. Just as new technologies in general and, more specifically, Web sites have evolved, so have Web courses. A Web course is just a subset of a Web site. So, the five developmental stages for adopting new technologies and for Web sites—denial, outsourcing, PowerPoint, execution, and integration—are completely applicable to Web-based training (e-learning).

Denial

When considering e-learning, an organization needs to look at its training and customers to see whether some or part of their training can be delivered over the Web. Many training organizations are made up of classroom trainers or subject matter experts brought in to impart information to others. Moving training to the Web represents a significant modification in how trainers do their job—and change can be frightening. Classroom trainers feel comfortable in front of a roomful of people, whereas they may be completely out of their element designing a Web course and delivering it to people thousands of miles away. Many of them, not surprisingly, resist moving even a small part of their training curriculum to the Web. Many organizations have avoided moving training to the Web not because the move couldn't move business ahead (not all trends and technologies are for every organization), but because of resistance from trainers and a lack of commitment from upper management. During the denial phase, most arguments center on a theme that the content does not lend itself well to Web-based delivery. This usually masks a fear of having to modify presentations based on face-to-face narration supported by bullet points to Web content that may be viewed without a trainer present to control the flow.

Outsourcing

When organizations decide to embark on e-learning, they look at ways they can outsource this new initiative.

In the absences of outsourcing, employees don't want to take responsibility for creating e-learning; they want to continue giving classroom training. Within the training department, a few trainers might volunteer to create e-learning. If someone does volunteer, everyone else is relieved, and they quickly funnel the e-learning projects to them. Obviously, at this stage e-learning has not been embraced by the organization. Although outsourcing solutions are also prevalent during the other phases of adoption, the difference is in the organizational attitude. At this stage the projects are outsourced to get e-learning deliverables off an employee's desk.

For e-learning, outsourcing manifests itself in a few different ways:

1. *The purchase of an LMS—a set of software tools that provide an array of functionality for e-learning needs:* Many companies start their e-learning initiative by purchasing an LMS. In so doing, they focus on infrastructure, not on solutions. An LMS may take IT a few years to install (because of all the integration needed with computer systems and with employee management systems). This gives trainers a few years before they need to embrace e-learning.

2. *The acquisition of a vendor's catalog containing generic courses:* Many times when an organization purchases an LMS, it also purchases a course catalog. Having fulfilled its e-learning requirements, it can now go back to its "real business."

3. *Outsourcing custom course development:* Within some organizations, soon there is a need to create company-specific courses. At this phase, they quickly identify an external course development organization, send them their PowerPoint presentation or training manual, and instruct them to contact them when they are done turning it into a course.

More recently, outsourcing manifests itself in yet another way: An organization saves a PowerPoint presentation as Flash, adds a narration track to it, and calls it e-learning. In the calls from organizations focused on solving their e-learning this way, typically the conversation goes like this:

> *Trainer:* I have a lot of PowerPoint presentations that I would like to turn into e-learning. Can I do that with your tool?
>
> *Designer:* Let's talk about your learner's experience. You can use your PowerPoint projects as the basis of your course. Here are some things I recommend that you do to create an effective e-learning course . . .
>
> *Trainer:* That sounds like a lot of work. I just want to press a button and get this deliverable off of my desk.
>
> *Designer:* What about the learner's experience?
>
> *Trainer:* I want something easy for me to use.

Obvious, such callers have not embraced e-learning as a method of meeting objectives and moving business ahead. Their goal is to minimize work on their end, not provide an effective learning environment.

PowerPoint

You can identify when a company starts embracing e-learning when trainers, product managers, human resources managers, and all other lines of business include e-learning as one of the ways to deliver information to their intended market. For example, product managers who are in the midst of a product rollout list press, advertising, Web, e-learning, and direct mail as delivery methods for getting the word out. Within their Web component, they may include creating a product page, providing a data sheet, and creating an e-learning course as methods of delivering product information to customers and prospects.

At this stage employees know about e-learning and naturally

include it as a standard business practice. The first step in organizational acceptance is to include mention of the trend or technology in planning sessions. The next step is a clear organizational understanding of quality. Specifically, is the level of execution supposed to move the organization's agenda ahead or just to fill in a check box as quickly as possible. In the case of a check box item, the deliverable is completed but is not effective and does not move the agenda ahead.

Execution

Execution shares many of the same processes as outsourcing. Organizations may install an LMS, purchase a suite of courses, and outsource development to external content houses. The difference is internal attitude. During the outsourcing phase, e-learning is a burden added to the other employee responsibilities. During the execution stage, creation of a successful course that meets business objectives is core to what they do. During the outsourcing phase, rarely does anyone include user surveys and try to identify how best they can modify a course for better learning. In the execution phase, managers and course developers look at course rollouts and discuss how the courses are being accepted and what they can do to tweak them to better meet business objectives.

Integration

At some point, creating e-learning courses is integrated into how the organization does business. At this stage the organization may have an LMS, a course catalog, courses built by professional course developers, and courses built internally. Management starts to pay attention to the satisfaction surveys for the content, and they develop an interest in tracking how much the courses are being used to promote sales or provide self-service support to the external customers or employees. Employees start using the courses as reference material in their daily work.

2.4 Fundamentals of Creating on the Web

To understand the fundamentals of creating good e-learning, you have to understand the fundamentals of creating good Web sites because a Web course is a subset of a Web site. That is, it contains Web site content and uses Web site technologies, but it is organized with a different flow. Most people can easily distinguish a Web site that works well from one that leaves them frustrated. Customers might not always understand the reasons that a particular Web site works while another one doesn't, but they don't have to. The organization does.

Certain fundamental principles make for a good Web site. The ones discussed in this section are included for one good reason: They work. Organizations have spent a lot of time and money creating Web sites that are intuitive to use. They want people to use their sites to access information; they don't want people to get frustrated and leave. When these basic Web principles are applied to e-learning, the courses work better, the learner has a better experience, and corporate goals and objectives are met. These principles work toward meeting those needs.

Training on the Web should be viewed as a subset of the Web. Any principle that applies to Web design also applies to e-learning design. The application of effective Web principles when creating e-learning increases the usability of your course.

The goal of a Web site is to create a positive experience for the visitor. Visitors want quick, accurate access to the information they seek. To achieve a good Web site, a series of best-of-breed characteristics should be included. These characteristics are found in *all* effective Web sites. The fundamental characteristics of any good Web site include:

A Simple and Clean User Interface: Less Is More

Don't overwhelm visitors when they come to your site. Even leading Web companies make this mistake. In the late 1990s, search engines focused on being a portal, Yahoo! being the largest. When you searched Yahoo!, you were so overwhelmed with their front page that you didn't know where to go or what to do. The page was covered with colorful pictures, animated advertisements, and Flash-based click-through graphics. Then Google came out with their search engine. Their front page was almost blank, containing just a place to input search terms. Their whole approach was extremely refreshing, not overwhelming. Google is now the leading search engine. They reminded everyone that a simple user interface can be a better solution, especially if it is supported by solid technologies that are transparent to the visitor.

Access to Any Information Within Three Clicks

Have you ever gotten lost on a Web site, unable to find what you are looking for? Have you ever had to click, and click, and click . . . and keep on clicking until you found yourself lost in some corner, finally abandoning the ordeal of finding information, or finding it once but getting lost on the site when you attempted to find it again. On the Web we quickly learn that visitors abandon their quest if it takes more then three clicks to get where they are going. A site where you can retrieve information in three clicks or less is referred to as a *flat site*. Creating such a site is similar to creating an outline, where you don't need to go deeper than three levels to find the material of interest.

Support of Global and Local Navigation

Good Web sites provide two levels of navigation to access information.

1. *Global navigation* allows the visitor to access important features or major areas of a Web site at all times.
2. *Local navigation* allows the visitor to move around the page or between pages.

Having two levels supports a flexible navigation path. It is important to provide key words that communicate areas of interest and then let visitors choose their path. Good Web content is accessed directly rather than through a fixed, linear path. Visitors should not be required to follow a defined path through information. Direct access allows customers to establish their own experience by choosing the information they want to access. Visitors who are forced to follow one path usually become frustrated and stop using the Web site as a resource.

No Bermuda Triangles

Bermuda triangles are deadends that leave visitors lost with no chance of ever finding their way back. Classic sources of Bermuda triangles include:

- Poor navigation
- Hard-to-find or nonexistent forward and back buttons
- Links that lead visitors off the site with no clear way of returning
- A lack of visual clues identifying the path that visitors took to get to where they are

A Sticky or Ping-Pong Web Site

A sticky Web site keeps a visitor engaged and on the Web site for more then a couple of clicks, whereas a ping-pong Web site sends the visitor off but provides a service that makes them want to come back often. A sticky Web site could be a video or a social networking Web site like YouTube or Facebook, whereas a ping-pong Web site would be a search engine like Google.

Rapid and Viewable Downloads

Visitors come to your Web site to access your content or applications. Therefore, rapid accessibility is paramount to the success of a Web site. Most people have little patience when performing daily activities; on the Web, they have even less. If a Web page does not instantly appear, visitors click out of it. If a graphic does not come up within 5 to 10 seconds, people get annoyed and leave. You need to formulate your Web pages so that they download quickly. That way, users don't get frustrated and leave.

In addition, creating content in HTML or XML is the simplest and most straightforward method of facilitating rapid accessibility. Web browsers are designed to display HTML and XML; content created any other way negates the power of the Web. HTML is so simple and powerful that when it is used to create a Web page, the page is *slim*; that is, it loads quickly and displays effectively regardless of the end user's display configuration.

HTML also makes for a better on-screen fit of the content. The Web is not a fixed-size paper printer. When printing, you know the size of the output sheet exactly. On the Web, you have no idea how big the end user's browser window is. Visitors may be coming to your Web site from a relatively low-resolution PDA or an extremely large, high-resolution screen. They may like to run multiple applications at once, so they minimize their browser size. Your Web pages must resize so that they work with these different browser configurations.

HTML enables your Web site to do that. If you change the size of a browser window, a picture does not move or scale, but HTML text moves, thereby reducing the amount of horizontal scrolling the reader has to do to read each line of text. This simple feature makes it easy to view text in a small or large browser window, on high- or low-resolution monitor, or even on a PDA or cell phone. Or, if a user has vision problems and changes the default font setting in the browser to 18 points and if the text on a Web page is written properly in HTML/XML, the text will display larger, even if the designer selected a smaller default font size.

HTML is also very powerful in other ways. Its power comes from:

- Browsers' ability to rearrange content for optimal display.
- The ability of search engines to read and archive it.
- The ability to narrate the content for blind readers (blind reader technology is programmed to identify and read HTML, so that readers with visual limitations can still use the material).
- Its compact format that results in very quick delivery to the end user's computer.

HTML is the most ubiquitously supported display language, although XML (a superset of HTML) is catching up quickly in its use. More importantly, search engines are created to read and catalog HTML/XML. This is beneficial not only to Internet Web sites but also to intranet sites. All the company information written in HTML/XML can easily be cataloged and retrieved from internal search engines called knowledge management systems.

The Ability to Work on Any Screen and Browser

Your site must work for everyone who comes to it. You never want your Web site to be a repellent. If visitors come to your Web site and it does not work for them because you never tested it on their browser, they will leave, never to return. Visitors have different size screens and use different browsers, and they will get very frustrated and leave your Web site if they need to horizontally scroll to read every line.

In addition to creating Web pages that work well regardless the size of the browser window, you need to also make sure your Web site works with all the different browsers out there, including Microsoft, Mozilla, AOL, and Safari. For example, Microsoft is the trickiest of all the browsers. Each version of Microsoft's Internet Explorer (IE) browser works differently. The IE V6 with Service Pack 2 supports multimedia and audio only if they are in the same directory as or below the page being displayed; all other versions of IE and all other browsers support the display of a graphics wherever they may be. So Web sites that work well in every other version of IE may not work right if the visitor comes into your site with IE V6 Service Pack 2. Also, most Microsoft tools are designed to work only with IE. Users who visit using Firefox or even an older version of IE may be unable to fill in forms or see certain content if it is built and delivered using Microsoft tools.

A "Look and Feel": "Branding" in Web Page Layout and Design

The look and feel of a Web site should mirror your organization's look and feel. *Branding* is the visual imagery you apply by using your logo and corporate colors on brochures, products, and packaging. Branding visually defines you, and your Web site should reflect your current branding. Our modern culture is very much keyed into branding, and this is one of the first things children learn as they start to read. McDonald's brand is the golden arches; Coca-Cola's brand is the white swirl on the red background. You don't need to read the label to know that a product comes from McDonald's or Coca-Cola; all you need to see is the brand image.

Creating clear and consistent branding is important for any Web site. To create a successful Web site, use your brand images as the basis for the design but extend it so that it is visible in such varied as PDAs. Effective organizations incorporate their current branding elements, including color scheme and logos, into the design and layout of their sites. An effective method for carrying branding over to the Web site is called *cascading style sheets* (*CSS*), the Web standard method of defining the look and feel of a Web page. CSS provides a couple of powerful advantages:

- It gives you complete control over a Web page, enabling you to control multiple pages of content from a single file, rather than setting up an individual file for each page of content. This feature makes it easier to ensure that all pages match in their look and feel, and so it simplifies changing the look of a site when a company updates its brand.

- Also, the same content can be made to look very different just by pointing it to a different CSS. Designers can change the look of a Web page without even touching the page. Thus one page can be displayed differently to different audiences. (See Figure 2.2.)

2.5 The Characteristics of Good e-Learning

Given that a Web course is a subset of a Web site, a good e-learning course includes all the core characteristics of a good Web site and builds on them to make it easy to learn the information presented. The same basic principles apply to e-learning as well as to Web sites.

Simple and Clean User Interface

Keep your e-learning course simple but informative. On the font page of your course, include the basics: a course name, a summary of the course, and clear navigation showing how to start the course. (See Figure 2.3.) The course summary is especially important to framing the course; learners get frustrated quickly when they do not have a clear idea what the course covers. The underlying principle is stated in the old training adage: "Tell them what you are going to tell them, tell them, and tell them what you told them." The summary tells them what you are going to tell them, and it should contain a one- or two-sentence overview or course objective.

Access to Any Information Within Three Clicks

The same four-level architecture found on effective Web sites should be applied to a Web course. (See Figure 2.4.) This so-called flat architecture provides access to any page found in a course within three clicks. The four levels are:

1. *Course pages*, which provide summary information.
2. *Chapter pages*, which also provide summary information that frames the content.

Figure 2.2 (a) One page, one CSS (Source: Picture courtesy of Eric Stoltz, www.ericstoltz.com); (b) same page, different CSS (Source: Picture courtesy of Rose Fu, http://www.rosefu.net/).

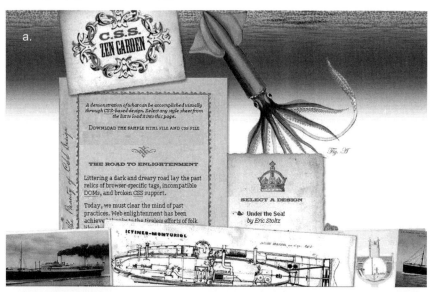

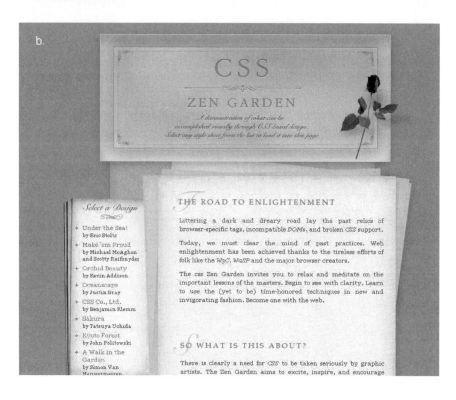

Figure 2.3 Front page of Web course.

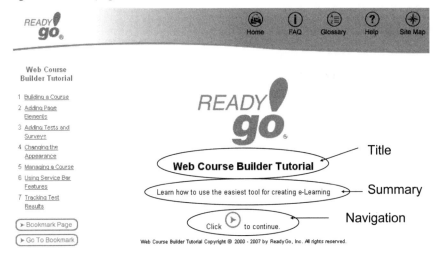

3. *Pages*, which are the core content found within a course.

4. *Subpages*, which are optional pages used to illustrate each point and which provide the greater depth of information, for either new or experienced learners.

As an example. let's say that in every hospital in the United States, all employees must take a hand washing course every year,

Figure 2.4 Web course architecture.

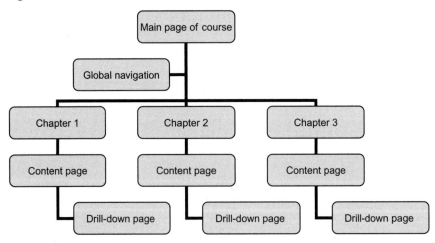

but they all come to the course with many levels of experience. A nurse with 20 years of experience does not need to rewatch a video on how to wash hands every year, whereas a new employee who has never worked in a hazardous environment should watch the video and review the six steps of proper hand washing. In addition, some hospitals may decide to allow hand sanitizers in specific areas of the hospital. Most employees are interested in understanding which areas of the hospital allow hand sanitizers and how to properly apply them. An epidemiologist may want to see the safety data behind the hospital's decision to allow hand sanitizers.

A Web course must be designed to meet all these needs.

- Course and chapter pages provide overview information that is likely to be helpful to most learners.
- Pages present the core information about hand washing and hand sanitizers.
- Subpages can be used to provide an optional video or step-by-step instructions for applying hand sanitizer.

Not all employees need to visit all four levels to get the most out of the course.

Support of Global and Local Navigation

Global and local navigation is very important for e-learners. (See Figure 2.5.) How to proceed with a course should be intuitively obvious.

- *Global* navigation elements are those that should be available at all times, including what the learner needs to terminate the course (depending on the environment, perhaps a link to another location or a course exit button). Other global features are buttons for the home page, frequently asked questions (FAQs), a glossary, a course map, and help.

Figure 2.5 (a) Global navigation; (b) local navigation.

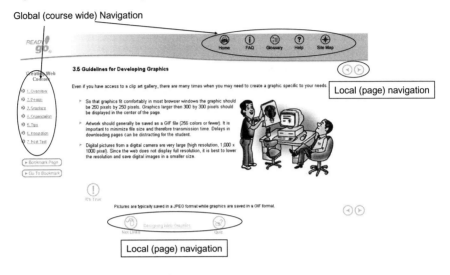

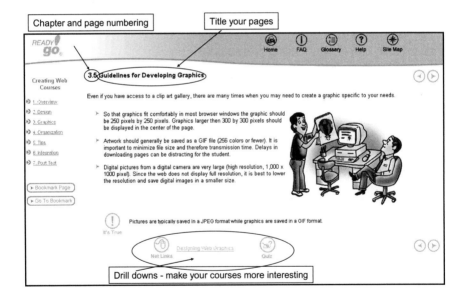

- *Local, or page, navigation* includes forward and back buttons, along with drill-down buttons. The navigation features should cue learners to identify where they are in the course.

Toward that end, chapters and pages should be numbered. Many learners need to know where they are in the flow of a course. When they pick up a book, the first thing they is to check out the last page number. While reading, they like to know whether they are a quarter, halfway, or three-fourths through the book. They have the same need when taking a course. Giving students clues that tell them where they are in the course and how much they have completed gives them control over their experience. It is better to have learners spending their time focusing on the content of the course rather than attempting to figure out where they.

No Bermuda Triangles

If your Web architecture is flat, yielding any information within three clicks in a convenient environment of global and local navigation, you should not have any Bermuda triangles in your course. However, another feature can create a Bermuda triangle: links. Links, of course, are beneficial in a course, but when creating a link, don't replace the current page with the linked-to page. Instead, bring the linked-to page up in a separate browser window.

Sticky or a Ping-Pong Web Site

A good e-learning course should be both sticky and ping-pong.

- It should be sticky when learners need to take the course because they stay on the course site for a considerable amount of time.

- It should be a ping-pong site after learners complete the course because it can be a good resource that learners can go back to. The use of a Web course as a resource is enhanced when all other good Web design concepts (flat layout, HTML/XML implementation, searchability, etc.) are applied.

Rapid Downloads

Learners have no more patience than anyone else. Here are a couple of ways to keep download time at a minimum:

- Run around your organization, taking pictures of employees at work, and then include the pictures in your course. Employees enjoy seeing people they know in a course, and this interest is a simple way to engage the learner. The caveat is that digital pictures tend to be very large. To make your courses download quickly, use a graphic tool like Corel Paint Shop Pro to save your shots in a lower-resolution format, thereby speeding up their download.

- The same goes for optimizing audio files. If you plan on using any form of multimedia, take the time to save the format in an optimized or smaller size so that they download faster. Microsoft Sound Recorder is one way to create audio files. The average size of a short audio file can be over 4 megabytes. You can easily lower this to 400 kilobytes (one-tenth the size) by choosing a different file encoding format (e.g., choose MP3 in the pull-down menu) in Microsoft Sound Recorder. The smaller size drastically changes the learner's experience. Instead of waiting a minute for the audio to load and play, the learner hears the audio when the page appears.

- Break videos into a series of short (two-minute) segments. Not only do these small clips download faster (because the user doesn't have to wait for the entire video to download before it starts playing), but they also give end users more control over what they are watching.

The Ability to Work on Any Screen and Browser

If you are working within your own organization, you know what technology people are using and can ensure that they can all view your course. If people are accessing your course from outside the organization, however, you can no longer control the browser they are using. There are several ways to deal with this issue:

- You can test run your course in all the different browsers to ensure it works.
- You can purchase a tool that automatically supports all the different browsers.
- You can implement your course in HTML or XML, which allows the course content to load quickly and accommodate the requirements of the browser.

You are going to spend a lot of time creating a course, and someone is going to spend a lot of money for you to do it. It would be a shame if learners can't access it.

A "Look and Feel": "Branding" in Web Page Layout and Design

A training course should support your organization's brand image. Include your organization's colors and logo in all courses.

2.6 Current State of Web Courses

The organizations that have successful integrated e-learning into the way they do business have a few similar characteristics:

1. The stakeholders and SMEs consider learning the material important and do not accept poor-quality training.
2. The organization cares about the learner's experience.
3. Course creators and their management have a desire to find out what it takes to create an effective course and how an e-learning course differs from a classroom training course.
4. They experiment with different approaches before investing large sums of money and time in a single large solution.

These characteristics might sound intuitively obvious, but they take a paradigm shift within many organizations.

With respect to Web-based courses, therefore, organizations are in every phase of the five stages of adopting new technologies, but many of them seem to get stuck in stage 2. There are probably many reasons for this state of affairs, but let's look at a few.

Trainers' Reluctance to Change

E-learning assignments are given to trainers. Trainers get their jobs because they are effective at standing in front of a group of people and presenting, not because they're good with computers. Most trainers don't currently have the skill set necessary to create e-learning, and they tend to do what any of us do when given a job that does not fit our skill set: They outsource, when possible, or use whatever means are available to make it easiest to get the deliverable off their desks. In these circumstances, the focus is on what makes the trainer's job easy. When pushed outside their comfort zone, trainers fail to focus on the corporate objective of providing effective training. The goal for organizations should be to move past stage 2 (outsourcing) and toward step 5: integration.

The Need for Feedback and Communication

There needs to be a feedback mechanism within the organization to ensure that training is effective and that it provides accountability for the quality of training. The feedback needs to be available where both learners and decision makers can report on the value of the training. Without this, there is no accountability, and poor training can flourish. (In future chapters we outline and detail the kind of information that organization members need to make informed decisions on what it takes to create and sustain an effective e-learning initiative.)

Creator-Centric Solutions

Interestingly, people rarely try to minimize the time it takes for learners to take training. Rather, they are more interested in minimizing the time it takes for course creators to create it. To get past the boredom factor, many course creators employ content heavy in visually stimulating elements, such as animated bullets and slide transitions, because these can be implemented quickly in tools like PowerPoint. However, such elements usually serve only as distractions (or points of pride for the authors) because they are not central to the content being presented.

Currently the favorite tool for getting a course off the trainer's desk quickly is PowerPoint-to-Flash converters with voice annotation. When asked about this choice, trainers typically say, "It's really easy for me [the course creator] to create." Not a word about the learner's experience. What is alarming is the imbalance between the time needed to create the content versus the time needed for the student to take it. A trainer in an organization of 2,500 employees creates a course that takes one hour to complete. It takes the course creator less than a half day to create a poor course, whereas it may take only a day and a half to create an effective course. A frightening large number of trainers don't want to spend one extra day creating decent courses, but they will allow the collective organization to spend 2,500 hours taking a poor course.

This attitude is the biggest problem in e-learning: a creator-centric attitude rather than a learner-centric one. There are a few reasons for it:

1. The organization doesn't know what to expect from e-learning.
2. Course creators are not evaluated based on the quality of courses they create.
3. The course creators don't know how to do any better, and the collective intelligence does not yet exist.

False Starts

Space Systems Loral, a satellite manufacturing company, started their e-learning initiative with a stock catalog of courses, which were barely used—a false start. They then moved to an internal content creation initiative that focused on a voice-annotated PowerPoint-to-Flash solution. Then they found out that employees were putting the course on auto run and returning when it was done. At the end of the 30-minute session, employees returned to their computers to answer any postcourse questions. Obviously this was not effective training—just another false start.

Often, false starts can be chalked up to fear of the unknown or of change. Think about it: When was the last time you did something new? How fearful are you of learning something new? Most people consider themselves bright and creative, but generally they are very fearful of change. Fear can show up in many ways: fear of learning something new, fear of change, fear of failing, fear of being measured or tested. Learning a new tool and learning a new way to present information can induce great fear, especially in organizations where training is viewed as a necessary afterthought. Learners don't want their time wasted on useless training. Many trainers want to use MS Office applications, especially PowerPoint, for their e-learning because they already know them and the perceived risks are very low. Since there is no learning curve, there is no fear of learning something new.

Consider a kindergarten-age child. In school she learns how to write her letters correctly, prereading skills (the sounds of letters and groups of letters), and the value of numbers. Out of school she is learning to ride a bicycle, play tennis, and roller skate. Everything she does all day long comes down to learning new skills. How many times do we as adults learn a new skill? How open are we to learning? How hard do we try to expose ourselves to new concepts, facts, or experiences on a daily basis? What is holding e-learning back and what is resulting in poor training is the common fear of learning a new skill.

In this case, the biggest fear seems to be of transferring what we know works in a classroom to the Web. The Web is a very different environment from our current world of classroom training, office applications, and e-mail. The MS Office technologies are all built around the paper publishing paradigm, which is two-dimensional and highly controlled. There is a defined width, height, and linear flow. The Web is three-dimensional (including the flow between pages) with an unknown target display size. Moving to this three-dimensional world, where the stand-up instructor is taken out of the picture, is a big step. This book gives course creators and managers the ideas and skills to span the knowledge breach between our current experiences and the huge opportunities offered by the Web.

2.7 Checklist

___ Identify which stage your organization is in with your e-learning initiative:

1. Denial?
2. Outsourcing?
3. PowerPoint?
4. Execution?
5. Integration?

___ Do the courses you build have:

1. A simple and clean user interface?
2. Access to any information within three clicks?
3. The support of global and local navigation?
4. No Bermuda triangles?
5. Stickiness or a ping-pong feature?
6. Rapid download?
7. XML or HTML?
8. The ability to work on any screen and browser?
9. Coherent Web page layout and design?

___ The organizations that have successful integrated e-learning into the way they do business have a few similar characteristics.

1. The stakeholders and SMEs consider learning the material important and do not accept poor-quality training.
2. The organization cares about the learner's experience.
3. Course creators and their management have a desire to find out what it takes to create an effective course and how an e-learning course differs from a classroom training course.
4. They experiment with different approaches before investing large sums of money and time in a single large solution.

3.0

Types of e-Learning

You can create e-learning in many ways. You can also save time and money—and produce a better experience for the learner—by identifying up front what type of e-learning best suits your resources and course goals.

In this chapter you will learn how to:

- Identify different types of e-learning.
- Learn how to create effective synchronous e-learning.
- Understand rapid and traditional asynchronous e-learning.
- Identify projects that are best suited for traditional e-learning and those best suited for rapid e-learning.
- Understand who develops traditional versus rapid e-learning projects.
- Understand what traditional and rapid courses look like.
- Select the tools used for e-learning.

3.1 Types of e-Learning

There are two main delivery modes for e-learning: synchronous and asynchronous.

- In *synchronous training*, students and teachers meet at a predetermined time for an instructor-led session.
- In *asynchronous training*, students use material made available through the Web that is complete enough to be used any time, allowing students to access it as needed.

Synchronous Training

Synchronous e-learning is similar to traditional classroom training. Typically the instructor and students are together on a conference call, log onto the same Web page, or log onto an on-line white board facility. PowerPoint is currently the most popular authoring tool for this kind of session, but it requires a delivery mechanism that converts it into Web-deliverable format. Most synchronous delivery systems include a shared whiteboard for viewing presentation content or for allowing instructors to share their computer's desktop with learners. The instructor controls what is shown, while the students listen to the lecture and view the whiteboard or slide passively from their computers. The instructor can hand control over to a student to make a diagram or a question or to permit the teacher to view the student's desktop. Most communication is done through message boards or instant messaging (IM). The instructor either fixes or entirely controls the content sequence.

Asynchronous Training

Asynchronous training is student guided. The content resides on the Internet, available to students when they are free to be trained—24 hours a day, seven days a week. The content must be complete enough in both breadth and depth so that self-study or referencing is possible. Therefore, presentation tools such as PowerPoint are poor choices. Without a live presenter, the talking points act as a weak skeleton, and the content contains only an outline of the topic.

A Comparison of Synchronous and Asynchronous Training

Both asynchronous and synchronous e-learning approaches have their advantages and disadvantages. (See Table 3.1.) Synchronous e-learning:

- Can provide the two-way communication between teacher and student that is often essential for proper training and evaluation, but it requires a live instructor and prearranged schedules.

- Has a time and cost benefit over classroom training because travel times can be eliminated; however, there is a loss of nonverbal communication that is sometimes needed for human evaluation and collaboration. Nonverbal communication takes place when people are in the same room watching each other's facial expressions, gestures, and behaviors, and it doesn't necessarily take place with e-learning.

- Is very effective when the material is rapidly changing because instructors can make changes and adapt their presentation while delivering the content.

TABLE 3.1 Synchronous Versus Asynchronous Features

Synchronous	Asynchronous
Content needs an instructor with a clear need for communication between instructor and student (instructor face time).	Content can stand on its own.
Instructor is available when students are available.	Course is available 24/7.
Students are not necessarily self-motivated.	Students need just-in-time training (available when they are, not when the instructor is available).
Instructor is changing content in real time (content is not finished).	Courses that can be used as a corporate resource, a reference for increasing productivity (e.g., can be accessed by a knowledge management system).

Asynchronous e-learning is different in many ways from synchronous training, and these differences need to be understood before the content is prepared.

- The main advantage of asynchronous e-learning is that the content is delivered when it is convenient for the student, at the student's pace, and, if done correctly, suitably for the individual's needs.

- Asynchronous e-learning does not require a live instructor. However, for effective use, the material needs to be much more engaging and must provide more depth of information.

- The content needs to be complete and interesting enough that the students can obtain the information they need for their training. When creating asynchronous e-learning, the course author needs to consider all reasonably possible questions that students would asked a live instructor and provide the answers before they have been asked. This allows the content to stand on its own.

Who Benefits from Synchronous and Asynchronous Training

Both types of e-learning courses have their place in the organizational training program. (See Table 3.2.)

TABLE 3.2 Synchronous Versus Asynchronous Courses

Synchronous Courses	Asynchronous Courses
Time-sensitive material	Shift workers
On-line seminar series	Training provided on a standard interval (e.g., once every six months
No budget or time to create asynchronous courses	Workers located around the globe
Personality-focused courses	Workers with unpredictable schedules
Easy assembly of the learners	Trainers with only limited availability
	Continuing need for just-in-time taining

Synchronous e-learning tends to be the most effective when there is a benefit from having a live person.

- Perhaps the content is time sensitive, and an expert, manager, or a public relations person needs to explain or disseminate it quickly and to be there to answer questions from the audience.
- Synchronous training might take the form of a seminar series in which an organization can reach groups of geographically dispersed participants for training.
- Synchronous training can also be used when an organization does not have the time or money to create an asynchronous course.
- Courses that are personality bound—where the SME brings the content to life or the message is largely motivational— are good candidates for synchronous e-learning.

Asynchronous delivery excels in training shift workers (hospitals, manufacturers, service centers), employees who travel, staff located in geographically distant offices, and personnel with unpredictable schedules (e.g., emergency workers, call centers).

- *Hospitals*, for example, are moving to asynchronous e-learning because they need to constantly train and retrain employees, many of whom fall into these categories. It is difficult to pull an emergency room nurse out of her shift for a scheduled training session; the busy times at the work-place are unpredictable, and the worker may be doing the late night shift when an instructor is typically not available. Asynchronous training lets nurses create their own training schedule around the flow of traffic in their departments.
- *Call centers* also have unpredictable loading schedules. Employees need to be trained on new products and proce-dures as they become available. Because of the variable load on call centers, it is difficult to plan training for all the em-ployees at slack times. An asynchronous course lets employ-ees control when they take training.

- *Salespeople* also benefit from the flexibility of asynchronous e-learning. Salespeople can be located anywhere in the world, making it difficult for them to take training at a pre-arranged time that is convenient for the instructor. They also tend to need just-in-time training and are notorious for having short attention spans. Salespersons may use an asynchronous e-learning course before or during a sales call to update themselves on the latest product specifications or service offerings. Often they need to present or answer a question about a product or feature they don't know very well. Asynchronous training provides them with an easy way to either refresh their memory or to learn the basics.

- *Volunteer organizations* that are continually signing up new members are good candidates for asynchronous training. If they have a lot of volunteers who sign up throughout the year, it may be difficult to schedule orientation courses. The organization can create a Welcome to Our Organization course that all new volunteers can take when they sign up.

3.2 Creating Effective Synchronous e-Learning

Personal Skills Needed

Synchronous e-learning is a natural application of skills that trainers have developed creating and presenting classroom training. The learning curve to create and conduct synchronous e-learning is shorter and more closely tied to existing trainer personality and approaches.

Synchronous e-learning is relatively easy for most organization to use because employees are already comfortable with conference calls. Trainers are also comfortable with the construction of their courses in PowerPoint. With synchronous e-learning the same familiar elements used in classroom training exist. We still have the trainer, the students, and the PowerPoint presentation. All we do is add a synchronous environment like WebEx, Adobe Acrobat Connect (formerly Breeze), or GoToMeeting.

What has changed is that the direct human connection is lost: specifically, eye contact, body language, and informal collaboration. Subtle verbal queues and group discussions are masked by the geographic separation between participants. Importantly, trainers lose the visual feedback indicating that a learner may be struggling with a concept because they can no longer see the student's face.

Tools Needed

Synchronous training makes use of many traditional tools.

PowerPoint is the tool of choice. Without eye contact and body language to engage the learner, the trainer needs to control the material. A good way of controlling the pace of delivery is to use such effects as so-called flying bullets (bullets that are added one at a time during a course). Timing the bullets to the presentation slows the learners down so that they don't get ahead of the trainer. Flying (or more precisely, hidden) bullets also keep the learner's eyes on the screen because human eyes naturally gravitate toward motion. However, the motion does not necessarily draw the user toward the content they can read. On the contrary, the motion can draw their attention *away* from content, thereby interfering with the flow of the presentation.

Poll and survey questions can also be used to engage the learner. In a classroom situation, effective trainers ask a question or survey the learners by asking for a show of hands in order to engage the class and get a better read of the audience. They can then adjust their presentation if necessary. In a synchronous environment a trainer still needs to engage the learners and read their audience. Without eye contact and body language, they can do this and increase their effectiveness by asking a poll or survey question every few slides. For this reason, synchronous training requires more upfront planning than in-class presentations because these questions have to be prewritten and entered into the on-line tool.

Questions can be forward looking—that is, asked before the material is presented. For example, in presenting the material in this chapter as a synchronous training course, the trainer could poll the learners before this section and ask: "Have you asked a forward-looking question when you have given a presentation?" By asking the question before presenting the material, they get the learners to think about the topic and engage them in the subject.

Poll or survey questions can also be used to get feedback that the trainer can use to focus the material. For example, before talking about delivery environments, the trainer can ask which environment the learners are using and then focus the material to closely address those environments, followed by discussions on the differences and similarities with other delivery systems.

Difficulties to Overcome

The most difficult aspect for a trainer giving synchronous e-learning is the lack of nonverbal feedback. Giving such a course is like talking to yourself. You sit at your desk, talk into the phone or headset, and look at the slides you are presenting. The only feedback from the audience is through polls, surveys, and chat rooms.

Synchronous training can also be difficult for learners, who might not feel as engaged as they would be if a person were standing in front of them and classmates were sitting around them. Many people feel free to multitask. It is really easy for a learner to disengage or only partially engage in a synchronous course because they are sitting at their desks on a computer with many distractions: their in basket, e-mail, and other software applications at their fingertips.

Synchronous training courses also lack informal collaboration. Many synchronous environments have mechanisms for collaboration between the presenter and the participants, or they may have collaboration tools like blogs, whiteboards, and IM for collaboration between participants. However, there is no easy mechanism for the open exchange of ideas in real time. What is missing from these sessions is the informal collaboration that takes place among people when they are physically together, watching each other trying to learn the material. Breaks, discussion groups, and informal conversations at tables can build teams and create synergies that would not exist otherwise. It is important to identify how important this type of informal collaboration is to the training session and to consider holding training in a classroom environment when information collaboration is necessary.

3.3 Rapid and Traditional Asynchronous e-Learning

Asynchronous content can be categorized into two different modes (see Table 3.3):

- *Rapid e-learning:* One to two people can typically develop rapid e-learning projects in one day to a week.
- *Traditional e-learning:* Traditional e-learning projects take a team of people two to six people to four to six months to produce.

Rapid and traditional e-learning have fundamental differences. The differences are obvious when taking a course and are remarkably obvious when creating that course.

TABLE 3.3 Differences Between Traditional and Rapid e-Learning Courses

Rapid e-Learning	Traditional e-Learning
Content rapidly changes or is updated frequently	Content is fixed or rarely changes.
Content may or may not be generic or have a short shelf life.	Content is generic or has a long shelf life.
Budget is limited or nonexistent.	Budget is large.
Information is of a just-in-time nature—a hot topic.	
Time for delivery is short.	Lead time to delivery is relatively long.
Existing content is being repurposed.	The content is original.
Subject can be explained in words.	Subject needs simulations or 3D models.

Rapid e-Learning

The name "rapid" usually refers to the time it takes to create the course, typically a day to two weeks. The most time-consuming issue when creating rapid e-learning is content. If the content is available, the time to create the course is short. Typically it takes about the same amount of time to create a rapid e-learning course as it would take to develop the same course for classroom training through a presentation tool. Rapid e-learning is to traditional e-learning what a segment on the evening news is to a major motion picture. Both are professionally produced and edited, but one is developed quickly for brief use, and the other has higher production values and a longer shelf life. When was the last time you watched an old news segment? When was the last time you watched an old movie?

The goal of effective rapid e-learning is to leverage the best practices of the Web to deliver content in a training format. The best tools to create rapid e-learning integrate instructional design and Web design features into the process. If the tool does not include these features, the course takes longer to create because the author must identify the elements needed and ensure that they are included. If you can use stock graphics and photographs, you also save time because you won't need to spend time and money creating graphics.

The "rapid" in rapid e-learning may also refer to:

- The amount of time that the user spends reading the material or revisiting it.
- The quick delivery from concept to the employee.
- The short cycle before the content needs to be updated.
- The rapid review cycle.

Traditional e-Learning

Traditional e-learning can be viewed as a Web-enabled version of computer-based training, focusing on providing a multimedia experience including elaborate animations and simulations. Due to its high production costs, one hour of traditional e-learning typically takes two to five professionals between four and six months to complete, and the resulting course is typically as graphically sophisticated as a movie or video game. Traditional e-learning teams, which might consist of writers, SMEs, instructional designers, programmers, and graphic artists, need to develop storyboards and scripts prior to implementation.

3.4 Projects That Are Best Suited for Traditional e-Learning

There are no absolute rules about which companies are better suited to rapid e-learning than for traditional e-learning. Conversely, some projects are better suited for rapid e-learning, and others are more effective as traditional e-learning. Very early in the process, a decision needs to be made as to whether a project is going to be developed using traditional or rapid e-learning techniques. Of course, before you decide on the category of the project, you need to understand the benefits and limitations of each approach. (See Table 3.4.)

Traditional e-learning courses are expensive and time-consuming to produce because they take a team of people many months to create. A traditional e-learning course, including simulations, may

TABLE 3.4 Nature of Projects Better Suited to Traditional Versus Rapid e-Learning

Rapid e-Learning	Traditional e-Learning
Content rapidly changes or is updated frequently.	Content is fixed or rarely changes.
Content may or may not be generic or have a short shelf life.	Content is generic or has a long shelf life.
Budget is limited or nonexistent.	Budget is large.
Information is of a just-in-time nature—a hot topic.	
Time for delivery is short.	Lead time is long.
Existing content is repurposed.	Content is original.
Subject can be explained in words.	Subject needs simulations or 3D models.

take 220 to 2,500 man-hours to create. Good candidates for traditional e-learning are:

- Projects that need extensive simulations, like industrial control systems (think flight simulators).
- Training with long shelf life, like a company backgrounder.
- Content that needs a lot of collaborative expertise to develop, like specialized graphic simulations or programming.
- High-visibility situations where a large external user base (such as the press) is expected to visit the content.
- Very generic topics where the content is not department or division specific, such as management training, financial training, or time management.

Keep in mind that it is quite costly to update traditional e-learning because they are typically built with complex tools or need someone to program the changes.

3.5 Projects That Are Best Suited for Rapid e-Learning

Projects that are best suited for rapid e-learning are those where the content or surrounding environment is rapidly changing, such as:

- New sales offers or special discounts.
- Regulatory requirements that are updated frequently.
- Customer support when new problems are discovered.
- Computer virus training as new exploit mechanisms are invented.

Industries with rapidly changing content include retail, banking, technology, pharmaceuticals, and health care. For example, a human resources department may need to update employee training on new or modified public safety regulations or explain how changes in a law may affect hiring or benefits. A call center may need to train employees on how to handle a myriad of issues that can quickly pop up, like a product recall, news-making announcements, or service outages.

Limited or short shelf life projects and products are also great candidates for rapid e-learning. A company does not actualize revenue if it cannot train the salespeople on the new offerings. By shortening the delay between product release and the availability of training, the organization can adjust quickly to changing market or competitive conditions. Rapid e-learning provides companies with a way to get the latest information to the people who need it most.

E-learning also provides an accessible format for disseminating information because it is not bound to an instructor's or a learner's schedule. For example, after an interest rate change, an e-learning course can provide a mortgage company with a quick and easy way to train the entire network of brokers on the changes, features, and benefits of the latest mortgage programs.

Many companies have projects or products that aren't viewed as fundamental to the company's strategy. Small projects and subreleases of major products usually don't get the funding of a full release or large project. Because it can cost up to ten times more to produce a traditional e-learning course than a rapid e-learning course, product managers who are responsible for add-on products usually don't have the budget to create a highly produced course. Similarly, they don't have the lead time needed for extensive production. Most importantly, a highly produced course may be unnecessary. If, for example, the product manager's products change on a quarterly basis, rapid e-learning provides the means to deliver courses that otherwise would not exist. These courses can be used to train salespeople, distributors, and customers on the features and benefits of new releases of the add-on projects.

In some industries or situations, new information hits the airwaves, and employees need to be trained immediately. One such case was the 2003 SARS scare. CHEX, a consortium of 43 American children's hospitals, realized that they needed to train (and certify) all 98,000 employees in their organization on how to identify and respond to SARS symptoms. CHEX went from identifying the need to having a rapid e-learning SARS course available to all employees in less than 48 hours.

Content Best Suited for Rapid e-Learning

The specific characteristics of content that lends itself to rapid e-learning include (see Table 3.5):

- Material that already exists in some other format.
- Subjects that can be explained in words and that don't require visual or physical experience to learn them—factual rather than subjective topics, a product versus a soft skill.

If some of the material already exists in a different format, repurposing it for rapid e-learning can be simple because the time necessary to identify and outline the content has already been spent. A benefit of the rapid e-learning process is that it is typically easy to update or modify an existing course. Many course creators use existing PowerPoint presentations as their source documents and:

- Create learning objectives.
- Match the learning objectives to what has already been created.
- Flesh out the skeletal slides by turning two or three words into complete sentences. Where appropriate, they add graph-

TABLE 3.5 Traditional e-Learning Versus Rapid e-Learning Projects

Rapid e-Learning	Traditional e-Learning
New human resources product offering	Company backgrounder
Quarterly product release	Customer training for a major product release
In-house product training	Brand training
Service training	Highly interactive graphic application (e.g., flight simulator)

ics, exercises, articles, links to resources, and tests to make the material interesting, and more importantly, complete.

In fact, a number of companies have learned that by providing customized e-learning on their products, they have saved their customers' trainers the costs of creating courses. For example, a software company that provides accounting software to medium-sized businesses is continually updating its products and services. At each customer location, all employees that access the software need to be trained. The material provided for training consists of features and benefits that can be listed and presented in multiple formats. Prior to the implementation of on-line training, internal and client training was done at the customers' sites. Product managers flew around the country, providing training to branch staff. Technical salespeople then scheduled and provided training at their customers' offices.

The cost of on-site training and the challenge of being able to deliver that training in a timely manner required them to find alternative solutions. The company's corporate trainers and product managers started off by using rapid e-learning techniques to develop courses for internal use by their sales staff. The on-line courses were very popular. Sales people found them so easy to follow and complete that they believed the training could be an effective shortcut in the sales process. The salespeople started giving their customers access to the internal training courses.

Once management realized that these courses were effectively supporting their sales process and were saving their employees time, they decided to create versions of the material for their customers. They then went an extra step: They decided to provide their technical sales staff with copies of their rapid e-learning tool and access to their training applications. The people in the field could then customize already produced courses for the unique needs of individual customers. Courses would contain only the features the customer purchased, and they were customized to the customer's look-and-feel, so that e-learning became a personalized service.

3.6 Development Needs of Traditional Versus Rapid e-Learning Projects

Traditional e-Learning Needs

Unlike rapid e-learning courses, a team of specialists is needed to create traditional e-learning. (See Table 3.6.) They create highly sophisticated interactions in which the content, graphics, and simulations are tightly integrated. Members of the team are technically proficient, allowing them to create complex interactions.

Most traditional e-learning teams consist of a team of at least five or more specialists.

- The lead person is a *project manager*, responsible for ensuring that the members are collaborating effectively to create the project schedule and to ensure the project meets its schedule.

TABLE 3.6 Development Needs of Rapid Versus Traditional e-Learning

Rapid e-Learning Needs	Traditional e-Learning Needs
SME and the tool in a one- to two-day learning curve	Power user tools in hands of graphic specialists, technically sophisticated users, in a two-week to six-month learning curve
Simple interactions	Possibly complex interactions
Can be created by one person	Team with advanced skills, e.g., programming, graphic design
Imports of graphics, clip art, simulations, and animations	Design and creation of graphics, simulations, and animations
Company acceptance at some level of e-learning	Low or no acceptance of e-learning (outsourcing of course production)
Conducive to a bottom-up initiative structure	Conducive to a top-down initiative structure
Pleasing but technically simple visual design	Integration of visual design (look and feel) as part of development process
Easy maintenance, updatability, and reposting	Need for power user to maintain, update, and repost

- Additionally, the team might have one or two *graphic artists* who are responsible for creating and executing all graphics found in the course. The graphic specialists use power user tools like Adobe's Flash, Dreamweaver, Photoshop, and Illustrator. These tools are graphically flexible, allowing an experienced graphic artist to create complex, interactive elements, but it takes months, if not years, to become proficient in these tools.

- Most teams have *programmers*, who assemble and code the course to ensure that all interactions perform correctly. The tools needed, along with others used to create sophisticated applications, need to be deployed by people with programming skills.

- An important member of the team is the *instructional designer*, who creates the course flow, learning objectives, and learning elements and who ensures that the course's interactions meet its learning goals.

- Every team needs an *SME*, who provides the subject knowledge and experience.

- A *writer* interviews the SME or uses source documents in collaboration with an SME to create the course content.

Because many organizations do not have the people with the background and skills needed to create traditional e-learning, courses are often outsourced to specialists in building traditional e-learning.

Because of their large budgets ($50,000 to $150,000 per course), traditional e-learning courses are driven by the top-down initiatives of senior-level management, who support and fund high-visibility projects. Corporate backgrounders, major product releases, and high-visibility services are the types of top-down, large-budgets e-learning initiatives.

Rapid e-Learning Needs

Rapid e-learning courses, rather than requiring a team of specialists, are usually created by a trainer or subject matter expert. (See

TABLE 3.7 Skills of Rapid vs. Traditional Development Teams

Rapid e-Learning	Traditional e-Learning
SME profile: Analytical thinker, able to deliver information in a structured form, like a journalist	Project manager
Optional: Artist to create project-specific graphics, simulations, or interactions	Graphic artist(s)
Optional: Instructional designer to bring	Programmer
Course up to the next level	Course developer
	Instructional designer
	SME

Table 3.7.) These courses typically take one day to a few weeks for an SME to create and cost $1,000 to $15,000 to produce. Rapid e-learning creators do not need to be as technically sophisticated if they use tools built for their use. In fact, SMEs and trainers rarely have the time, patience, or background to learn to use sophisticated graphic tools. They use a rapid e-learning tool that allows them to assemble and publish a course quickly. Whereas a traditional e-learning course is a simulation or virtual world, a rapid e-learning course might include an interaction on only one of its pages.

Part of the definition of "rapid" is that the course can be built by the employees either who have the direct knowledge or who have access to the person with the knowledge. Thus, these course development projects tend to be bottom-up initiatives; that is, they are driven by individual contributors or people within the organization with a direct need. For example, a training course that explains evacuation procedures in case of a fire may be driven by a facilities manager. She may have been tasked to ensure that all employees, including new hires, are aware of what they need to do when the fire alarm goes off.

Thus, rapid e-learning courses are typically created by a trainer who is tasked to turn existing classroom training into e-learning or by an SME responsible for transferring knowledge.

Therefore, course creators will have more success if they can touch on all the subjects handled by the specialists without being specialists themselves.

Nor do course creators need to be the kinds of specialists needed for traditional e-learning training. Rapid e-learning courses can utilize canned graphics, existing illustrations, and photographs taken around the office instead of custom-built elements. When the need arises, creators may access a graphic artist who can illustrate new concepts, and some organizations have instructional designers in their training department. These instructional designers can work with the trainers to help them bring the courses up to the next level. Course creators can also purchase a software package that creates simple, generic interactions. The generic interaction software usually can be modified in only a limited manner to give the interaction a custom look. For example, the developer may purchase a tic-tac-toe game that allows them to modify the game's colors and change the graphics used for the Xs and Os. Rapid e-learning courses therefore do not need to be outsourced in their entirety.

Training organizations that are looking to hire someone specifically to create rapid e-learning courses have been successful when they hire print reporters with a graphic eye. Reporters work well because they have good writing and interviewing skills, and they are comfortable dealing with layout issues The need to have them do custom programming can be eliminated by using generic interactions provided by the rapid e-learning software or simply by avoiding them. (Custom interactions are generally considered unnecessary for rapid e-learning content.)

Thus, four skill levels are associated with rapid e-learning development (see Table 3.8):

1. The basic skill level is where the SME takes existing material and turns it into a course, probably using an existing Power-Point and fleshing out the content.

2. To bring a course up to the next level, the SME adds graphics, simulations, movies, and pictures.

TABLE 3.8 Author Skill Levels for Rapid e-Learning

Course Developer	Skill Level
Level one	Takes knowledge and creates a course.
Level two	Can change graphics, colors, add in clip art.
Level three	Collaborates with graphic artist to bring courses to life.
Level four	Collaborates with instructional designer to make the course more effective.

3. At the third level, the SME collaborates with a graphic artist and creates additional graphics that support the material.
4. At the highest level, the SME works with an instructional designer to ensure that the course is presented in the most effective format for optimal learning.

Given its stripped-down needs, rapid e-learning has a lot to offer large e-learning groups. For example, Telefonica, a $60-billion-a-year telecommunications company, tasked its e-learning division, Educaterra, with increasing e-learning production from 50 courses a year to 500, with no major increase in budget. Educaterra was accustomed to producing traditional e-learning courses, each of which typically took a team of four to six course developers about four months to produce. Management at Educaterra realized that they needed to rethink e-learning to accommodate a tenfold productivity increase. They solved their problem by creating two groups: (1) a traditional e-learning group, and (2) a rapid e-learning group, dubbed their Content Factory. Management then categorized all the projects into two tracks.

1. The courses that had a long shelf life, needed extensive simulations, and required high production costs were given to the traditional e-learning group.

2. The courses that needed a fast turnaround, were more content focused, and could stand on their own with simple simulations or graphics were given to the Content Factory.

The traditional e-learning group had 80 employees, and the Content Factory consisted of four people. The Content Factory course developers needed a different skill set because their team was so much smaller than their traditional counterpart; in fact, they all had a background in journalism. Educaterra understood the analogy between traditional/rapid e-learning development and a major movie/the nightly news. One relies on an extensive production effort, long lead times, and a specialized team of highly skilled graphic artists and designers. The other is quickly produced, narrative based, and reliant on a reporter to create, edit, and produce.

Educaterra's e-learning division achieved production of 500 courses a year. The traditional e-learning group produced 50 courses a year, and their Content Factory produced 450. Obviously, the two kinds of courses were very different, but the delivered the information and achieved their objectives.

Whenever you need to create a new course, your first task is to decide which approach should be used. Once you know the differences between traditional and rapid e-learning, identifying the appropriate technique is straightforward. To do so, ask only a few simple questions, as shown in Table 3.9. Based on the project, circle the best-match answers for the project, and which approach to use will become quickly evident.

3.7 What Traditional and Rapid e-Courses Look Like

The look and feel of the two types of courses can be very different. Let's look at and compare few screen snapshots to get a feel for the features of each type of course and how they might work with your content.

TABLE 3.9 Determining the Appropriate Type of e-Learning

Question	Type of course
What's the budget?	Big budget: Traditional Low budget: Synchronous or rapid
What's the shelf life?	Long shelf life: Traditional or rapid Short shelf life: Synchronous or rapid
When does it need to be ready?	Today: Synchronous Within a month: Synchronous or rapid In six months: Synchronous, rapid, or traditional
Can the subject be explained in words or pictures?	Rapid
Do we need complex graphics or simulations?	Traditional
Do we need an instructor to bring the material to life?	Synchronous

The Traditional Course Look

The three screen snapshots in Figure 3.1 are of courses built using traditional e-learning techniques. You can see how visually powerful even a screen snapshot is. Telefonica's traditional e-learning group created the following three courses. In each of these courses they created graphically heavy, virtual worlds:

- Figure 3.1a shows a virtual world created to teach people how to create e-mocion (read "e-motion") Web pages.
- Figure 3.1b shows a virtual world created to train employees how to navigate through Telefonica's product and service offerings.
- Figure 3.1c is from a series of simulations created to train employees on how to effectively handle different types of meetings.

Figure 3.1 Simulation environments in a traditional course.

a.

Virtual world to train employees how to navigate through Telefonica's offerings

b.

c.

Simulations on how to handle different types of meetings

The Rapid Course Look

Courses that are produced with rapid techniques can also be visually attractive and can include interactions and simulations. Perhaps a key to differentiating the different types of courses is that in traditional ones, the environment is the foundation of the course, whereas in rapid courses the environment is secondary to the textual content. Even so, the difference is obvious. Rapid e-learning courses tend to be more focused on words and reading and less on creating a visual virtual world.

- Figure 3.2a is a screen capture from a course produced to help employees learn how to better mange work relationships.
- Figure 3.2b is from a course produced to teach employees how to create actionable items.
- Figure 3.2c is from a quick guide created to explain available employee training programs.

3.8 Tools

No single tool can be used to create all the different elements found in e-learning. The creation of effective e-learning courses requires a number of tools and proper judgment about how and when to use them appropriately. This is not different from how we work in our desktop environment. Most SMEs, for example, currently use different tools to execute different functions: Word to create documents, Excel to create spreadsheets, PowerPoint to create presentations, and Project to create schedules. An SME would consider it ridiculous and think less of a coworker who wrote a document using PowerPoint, created a spreadsheet using Word, or composed a presentation in Excel. Even though you could figure out how to create each of these types of documents in the inappropriate tool, the time it would take and the resulting solution would be less than optimal.

So one of your first tasks is to find a kit of tools that work for

Figure 3.2 Rapid e-learning content environment.

a.

Telefonica course on managing work relationships

b.
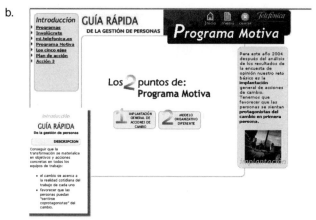
Telefonica training to teach employees how to create actionable items

c.

Telefonica Quick Guide to Employee Training

you. This is one of the more difficult steps you must take when moving to the Web. Most people are resistant to change, and a new tool may represent a daunting amount of change. A new delivery environment (the Web) presents even more of a challenge. However, using the wrong tool for e-learning or taking a pre-Web tool and using it to create Web courses only creates a subpar experience both for the course author and, more importantly, for the audience.

Presented another way, you might have a tool that can simply save your existing material in a Web-deliverable format. Alternatively, it might take you 40 additional hours to identify and learn a new tool designed for a Web environment. However, the extra time investment will result in a more positive experience for the end user. Suppose, for example, that you use this tool to create a one-hour training session to be taken by 1,000 employees. If the experience for the users is bad—nobody sticks around long enough to read or remember the material—1,000 wasted employee hours would be the result. Don't you think spending 40 hours up front so that 1,000 hours are spent productively is worthwhile?

This theory was tested at Telefonica. Senior management asked Educaterra why they were spending so much time creating courses when they could just take the existing PowerPoint presentations, save them as Flash, voice-annotate them, and put them on-line. The training group management at Educaterra felt that repurposed PowerPoint would create a suboptimal experience, but they needed to convey this concept to their "customers"—management. They decided that the best way to explain this was to conduct an experiment so that the results would tell the story. Educaterra created a compliance course that 20,000 employees needed to take. They asked two employees to create the same course in parallel, using the same PowerPoint presentation as the source document. They also created a test and survey that both course creators would use.

- One course creator was given a PowerPoint-to-Flash tool and was allowed to annotate the slides with audio.
- The other course creator was given ReadyGo Web Course Builder, a tool that moves Power Point slides into the tool,

adds Web design to the material, and steps the course
creator through the process of adding instructional design
to create the course.

Both course creators were familiar with the tools they were using,
and it took both of them a similar amount of time to create their
courses.

The PowerPoint course was given randomly to 10,000 employees, and the Web course was given to a different random set of
10,000 employees. The results were astounding. The employees
who received the Web-based course scored 20 points higher than
the employees who were given the voice-annotated PowerPoint.
Additionally, the employees who received the Web-based courses
gave 40 percent higher satisfaction feedback in the postcourse survey. Educaterra management had believed that Web design and instructional design would make a difference, but they were surprised
at much of a difference it made. From a corporate point of view,
what manager would want employees who score 75 percent on
courses over employees who score 95 percent? The difference is
between a C-grade employee and an A-level performance. What
this case really showed is that instructional design and Web design
make a difference in e-learning. If an organization is serious about
creating Web courses, it has to build these courses using the appropriate tools.

Before choosing a tool, course creators need to identify the
type of course they will be creating and what features will be in the
course. Only then can they choose the appropriate tool.

Traditional e-Learning Tools

Traditional e-learning developers use Power User tools, which are
designed for graphic artists, Web designers, programmers, and instructional design experts. Learning how to proficiently use these
tools typically takes weeks, if not months. These tools usually present the course creator a blank WYSIWYG (what you see is what
you get) screen that provides them with graphic flexibility. How-

ever, the WYSIWYG screen does not provide the developer with structure or queues about what elements (such as navigation) they need on their page. The developer therefore needs a lot of experience to use the tool to create all the parts of the environment. In creating a course, traditional course creators need to make a storyboard, do the layout, and design the course. Consequently, courses produced with traditional e-learning tools, such as Macromedia's Flash and Dreamweaver, have high production costs.

Rapid e-Learning Tools

When e-learning is in the hands of the SME or trainer, the tools need to be simple to use. Most importantly, the tools must be focused on content rather than on graphic layout. Tools like the ReadyGo Web Course Builder produce multilevel courses but do not require a graphic or design background. They also allow for a quick adoption curve. Most SME or trainers create a course, attend to other business, and five months later return to the tool to create the next course. SMEs and trainers do not have the time or experience to create storyboards, graphic layouts, and delivery environments. They may feel comfortable surfing the Web but do not have the experience to design a Web site. So a rapid e-learning tool must have a lot built into it. It must be as easy to use as PowerPoint but have storyboards, Web design, instructional design, and flexibility so that the trainer can take advantage of the capabilities offered by the Web.

Graphic and Simulation Tools

Separate from the authoring tool are *graphic and simulation* tools. These tools are used in rapid e-learning to create interactions that professional graphic artists would typically build in Flash and Dreamweaver. The tool developer creates generic templates with built-in interactions; then the developer is allowed to make minor modifications to the templates, such as changing the displayed text. A few popular simulation tools are Captivate, Camtasia, and

ViewletBuilder—all screen snapshot tools. They record screen movements, allowing an SME or trainer to create a simulation of events that happen on a screen. They can also be used to show people how to use a computer application.

Other options include *interaction tools* like Raptivity or Hot Potatoes. These tools have a catalog of already created games and interactions that can be added to a course. You can also add an avatar to a Web page using a tool like NOHA, so that instead of a talking head or just audio, a cartoon figure does the talking.

Synchronous e-Learning Tools

To successfully host a synchronous e-learning session, you need at a minimum a conference line and tool like WebEx, Citrix Go-ToMeeting, or Adobe Acrobat Connect. Because synchronous e-learning sessions are similar to classroom training and the material does not need to stand on its own, a presentation tool like PowerPoint can be used for authoring. These conference systems, however, typically require that all participants in the training install a client-side application on their computer so that they can access the central or shared desktop.

3.9 Checklist

__ The types of courses best used for these purposes are as follows:

   1. Rapid e-learning checklist:
      - Content rapidly changes or is updated frequently.
      - Content may or may not be generic or has a short shelf life.
      - The budget is limited or nonexistent.
      - The information is just-in-time in nature, a hot topic.
      - A quick delivery time is needed.
      - Existing content is being repurposed.
      - The subject can be explained in words.

2. Traditional e-learning checklist:

- Content is fixed or rarely changes.
- Content is generic or has a long shelf life.
- The budget is large.
- The lead time is long.
- The content is original.
- The subject needs simulations or 3D models.

__ Success factors:

1. Rapid e-learning:

- SME can use the tool; it should be as simple to use as PowerPoint and Word, with a one- to two-day learning curve.
- Produces content that is easily deployed.
- Does not require a team of people to create a course.
- Course creator can import graphics, clip art, simulations, and animations.
- Company understands the value of e-learning (the cost, time, accessibility, savings of moving classroom training to the Web).
- Works well in a bottom-up initiative structure.
- Visual design (look and feel) is supplied by company; the course developer is not involved.
- Courses can be easily maintained, updated, and reposted.
- Works well in a bottom-up initiative structure.

2. Traditional e-learning:

- Power User tools are needed, in hands of graphic specialists and other technically sophisticated users, with a two-week to six-month learning curve.
- May include complex interactions, high bandwidth content, plug-ins.
- Needs a team with advanced skills, such as programming, graphic design, instructional design.
- Course creator creates graphics, simulations, and animations.
- Company has not necessarily embraced e-learning.

- Works well in a top-down initiative structure (large budgets, large projects).
- Visual design (look and feel) is integral part of development process.

___ Development team:

1. Rapid e-learning project:

    - SME profile: Analytical thinker, able to deliver information in a structured form (like a journalist).
    - Optional: Artist to create any project-specific graphics, simulations, or interactions.
    - Optional: Instructional designer to bring course up to the next level.

2. Traditional e-learning project:

    - Project manager.
    - Graphic artist(s).
    - Programmer.
    - Course developer.
    - Instructional designer.
    - SME.

___ Skill levels for rapid e-learning course creation:

1. Level one: Takes knowledge and creates a course.
2. Level two: Additionally, can change graphics and colors, add in clip art.
3. Level three: Collaborates with graphic artist to bring courses to life.
4. Level four: Collaborates with graphic artist and programmer (database) to bring additional functions to a course.

___ Differences between synchronous and asynchronous delivery methods:

1. Synchronous:

    - Content needs an instructor; there is a clear need for communication between instructor and student (instructor face time).

- Instructor is available when students are available.
- Students are not necessarily self-motivated.
- Instructor is changing content in real time (content is not finished).

2. Asynchronous:

- Content can stand on its own.
- Course is available 24/7.
- Students need just-in-time training (available when they are, not just when the instructor is available).
- Courses can be used as a corporate resource, a reference for increasing productivity (e.g., can be accessed by a knowledge management system).

Web 2.0

About every 10 years, there is a so-called new and emerging trend in the technology industry. This chapter reviews the latest trend in technology, dubbed Web 2.0.

By the end of this chapter, you should be able to:

- Understand the basics of Web 2.0.
- Identify what types of application services are found on a Web 2.0 site.
- Describe the Long Tail.
- Explain mashups.
- Explain how to enlist end users to add value.
- Define the concept of Intel Inside.
- Describe how to provide services above the level of a single device.
- Use social networking.

4.1 The Basics of Web 2.0

The 1970s brought us mainframes. The 1980s brought us personal computers (PCs) that morphed into the client-server market of the late 1980s. The mid-1990s gave us the Internet. This decade is bringing us Web 2.0.

Let's take a step back and remember what the Internet looked like in the 1990s. Companies had Web sites that provided information about the company, its products, and in many instances, merchant sites where you could purchase products. Internet companies focused either on selling a new product or service or on becoming a portal (information broker) or integrator. *Portals* are central locations where visitors with specific interests go to obtain information collected from other sources. As the Internet matured, the development of existing technologies made it easier to provide more services. For example, visitors started being able to customize the portal pages assigned to them to customize these services to their tastes. As the technologies matured, new applications became viable and available. The old applications are still available and relevant, but the new applications are what Web 2.0 is about.

Keep in mind that each new trend does not mean the demise of the previous one. We still have mainframes, PCs, servers, workstations, and Internet browsers. However, new trends layer on top of the older, established technologies and enable us to provide new services to a growing user base.

- In the 1980s the technologies of the day made it easier to mass market, that is, to send out mailings to a large group of people.

- The 1990s Internet explosion allowed us to mass customize, that is, to provide services to people with similar interests.

- Today's trends let us mass personalize, that is, give people with specific (niche) interests access to products, services, or like-minded people.

The latest trends in technology were collectively dubbed Web 2.0 by Tim O'Reilly and Dale Dougherty of MediaLive. They saw how the Web was changing how we live and work. More importantly, they saw that the new Internet applications were different from previous ones. They looked at these differences and identified six specific characteristics of the newer applications. The six new trends they identified as Web 2.0 are:

1. Application services.
2. The Long Tail.
3. Mashups.
4. Enlisting end users to add value.
5. "Intel Inside."
6. Providing services above the level of a single device.

4.2 Application Services

Application services are a new and important trend in technology. In the past, PC users at home installed software locally on their computer to carry out the tasks of interest to them. They still have software, but now they also have access to many application services.

An application service runs outside the end user's computer. Instead of installing and managing software, an application service allows Web site visitors to access applications without having to install or manage new software. The benefit for consumers is simplicity. They can access new applications without having to download, install, and maintain software. An application service can replace existing software in the same way that Google Mail wants to replace the mail client on your computer. Google Mail would replace locally installed applications like Microsoft Outlook or Mozilla Thunderbird.

An application service can replace the old way of doing things, just as MapQuest and Google Maps have supplemented the paper street guides. Sometimes application services are new applications we never thought we needed, like Wikipedia, where one now has access to an encyclopedic level of information on almost any subject.

As with all technology trends, new technologies usually augment but do not entirely replace existing technologies. For a number of reasons, people still want to buy software and run it on their PCs.

- Many applications, like those used to develop graphics, need a lot of interactivity between the creator and the application. Current Web-based technologies are slow and cumbersome when used as the basis for these types of applications. If you are going to work with a 50-megabyte graphic or video file, you have the fastest access if the file is stored and manipulated locally on your computer. If you have to download, modify, and upload the file to a central, remote server, the timing is much slower. So it is still best to use your PC or Mac when using applications like Adobe Illustrator or PaintShopPro, for example, rather than using a Web-based graphic application.

- Security is another reason people shy away from using Internet-based applications. If you are creating documents that are being saved on someone else's hard drive, think long and hard about security. Questions to ask before creating documents that reside on someone else's hard drive are:
  - Will the company sell my data?
  - Will it hand the data over to a government if asked?
  - How long will they store the data?
  - Who else has access to the data?
  - Will they sell my private data to other services?
  - Do I have to keep paying them so that they don't delete it?

- Finally, before relying on applications services, consider the environment. Questions to ask are:
  - How accessible is the application during travel?
  - Does it work well even with poor or spotty Internet service?

Partly as a result of these concerns, people tend to use applications over the Internet that are not the traditional software products they have installed on their PCs, that is, applications that create personal files. The new applications provide access to information you never had access to before. For example, one new application supplies research on for-sale house listings; you input a zip code and get access to the prices, pictures, maps, and specifications of homes in that area.

Information technology (IT) departments are also using application services. From a business point of view; application service providers (ASP) provide what is referred to as hosted solutions, alternatively called on–demand applications. At some level these types of services have been around for a long time. Back in the 1960s, 1970s, and 1980s, IT departments time-shared applications; that is, they paid outside agencies to host, manage, and run corporate applications. They did this because the cost of hardware, software, and IT people was high; so sharing a mainframe was more economical for certain applications. However, IT departments are savvy technology users. They are good at figuring out the total cost of ownership and deciding which is economically more responsible: to purchase the software and hardware and then hire the people to run an application or to pay an outside agency to host it.

Employees are accustomed to using application services for corporate functions. For example, IT departments traditionally run e-mail, conference room scheduling, and financial applications. End users access IT applications without having to install their own copies of the software. What is new from an IT point of view is that in the past IT did not have a choice as to whether to purchase software or sign up for a hosted solution. IT now can look at mundane applications, like e-mail and room scheduling, and at core applications, like financial applications, and decide which ones vendors should manage and which ones need to be managed in-house.

Most corporations choose to host core applications, those—that are core to their business, like financials—and they are willing to outsource peripheral applications, like conference room scheduling. The biggest change for IT departments is the change in vendors. In the past, most vendors offered only a customer-installed solution. Now, most are offering either customer-installed services, hosted services, or both.

4.3 The Long Tail

The Long Tail consists of the portions of the bell curve that reflect smaller markets. Most marketing bell curves consist of a core (representing the bulk of the market) with a tail at each end (representing specialized segments of the customer base). In Figure 4.1, sections 1 and 3 represent the tail of the bell. From a marketing point of view, the core customers are found at the center of the curve, by section 2. Most successful business and all large businesses focus on core customers because they are the largest group of buyers. Businesses can grow large and successful by providing 80 percent of product and services to 80 percent of the market. That does not mean business opportunities do not exist in the 20 percent of the market not being served (the tails). These portions of the market

Figure 4.1 The long tail of the Bell Curve.

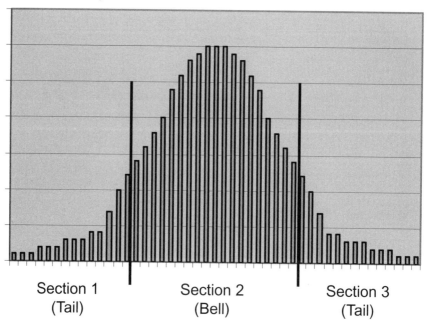

Section 1	Section 2	Section 3
(Tail)	(Bell)	(Tail)

are typically ignored because the large companies focus on economies of scale and ease of access.

The so-called tails can be pretty large, such as in regional air travel. In some industries the products, services, and people represented by the tail are not served, typically because the tail is very long. A long tail represents a very diverse, segmented market, that is, the 20 percent represented by the tail might not be similar or want similar products, they might be geographically difficult to reach, or it might be difficult to identify what they want. From a business perspective, the tail represents a lot of cost to reach an extremely small market. If they all want is something different, providing a solution for all of the members of the tail might not be economically feasible.

The goal in the past with mass marketing and mass customization was to provide more and better products and services to the center of the bell. Nowadays, focusing on the long tail is a move to mass personalization—providing niche services to a niche market. With the Internet making it economically feasible to reach many underserved markets and with so many people on the Internet, marketing to people in the tail of the bell curve has become much easier. That is, customers with specialized needs can now find smaller companies serving their needs through portals and search engines.

A good example of servicing the tail is Netflix, a video rental company that uses the Internet to let customers order videos. Before Netflix, most people rented videos from local, neighborhood stores like Blockbuster. People walked into a Blockbuster store, found a video they liked, and took it home to watch. Due to store size, Blockbuster limited its selection to the top 1,000 videos of interest. If old or independent (indie) videos were not being rented frequently, they lost their shelf space to a video that could be rented. This was fine for most of the market. But people who liked foreign, old, or indie films were not served well by the local video stores. Instead of having a physical, neighborhood store with videos on the shelves, Netflix has an on-line catalog and large warehouses. Since they are not constrained to shelf space, their catalog can be unlimited.

People who are interested in unusual films, like foreign, indie, or old films, can find them in the on-line catalog and order them. Many times people who watch the top movies also might want to watch a foreign, indie, or old movie. Most of the movies Netflix rents are in the core of the bell, but what distinguishes their service and makes people want to use it is that they can access the tail of the bell.

4.4 Mashups

Another trend in modern applications, a mashup site takes content from two or more services and combines them into a Web page or service. The combination of the content from the various sites and services can also be offered as a service. This ability to layer is very powerful, providing benefits to multiple participants: The underlying Web site now receives more visitors and maintains its value by allowing new services to use it. The end user gets information combined from several sources without having to separately visit each of those.

New services like mashups do not need to recreate the wheel; they can aggregate existing services and add their own services to create new ones. An example of a mashup is Zillow.com, a Web site that allows you to choose a street address and see the price for the house. It layers many existing technologies on top of each other to create a better service, using existing map Web sites, Real Estate Multiple Listing Services (MLS) listings, and city records. By combining these different services, it creates a new, enhanced service. Home buyers tell you that, when they are considering purchasing a house, it is really nice to look at an aerial map and see the prices of all the houses in the neighborhood. They like to see which houses on which streets are for sale or have sold, as well as what the prices were. Services like Zillow.com give home buyers transparency and data, two factors much needed to make an informed decision.

4.5 Enlisting End Users to Add Value

Web sites that sell products and services are always looking for ways to distinguish themselves from other sites. Using end user comments, blogs, and critiques has turned out to be an effective way to add value.

Vendors of generic products have found that by making it easy to let visitors make comments on their products or services, they can increase the value of their site and differentiate their services. Visitors to a Web site are interested in what others have to say about a product or service.

This is not a new phenomenon. Zagat, a company that rates restaurants, hotels, and nightlife has been using the so-called man-in-the-street interview for years. For over 25 years Zagat has been asking patrons of restaurants to rate their restaurant experience. They then average many people's ratings to create a measurement for each restaurant. The real value is that when you get a large group of people commenting on the same place, you don't get stuck with individual biases, and you wind up with the collective wisdom of the masses.

On the Internet it is easy for visitors to leave a review and rate products and services. Visitors coming to a site can use existing reviews as a guide to help them make a decision as to whether to purchase the product. In theory this should make it more comfortable for people to purchase a product or use a service. Web sites that sell products or services have found that this type of user content creates a unique service and an excellent way to distinguish their sites from others. The real bonus for these Web sites is that they have enlisted end users to add value to their Web sites. End users feel empowered, prospects appreciate the feedback, and Web sites create a loyal customer base. From the company's point of view, all they need to do is to supply the technical infrastructure for customers to create a comment and for visitors to read these comments. The true added value is the commentary: All these comments are free. The biggest caveat for Web sites is that the product or service must meet expectations, or this vocal group of Web commentators will provide negative feedback.

Amazon was one of the first Web sites to take advantage of this phenomenon. They democratized book sales by allowing visitors to review, rate, and comment on books. Where you buy a book doesn't matter because books are commodity items and you receive the same product in all cases. What does make a difference is your experience purchasing that book. Customer comments create a personalized and extended experience, just as a good salesperson in a brick-and-mortar bookstore can recommend books to customers. The added value of having thousands of customers comment on a wide range of products creates unique value that is difficult for the competition to replicate.

Some Web sites, those in the business of end-user opinions, are made exclusively of end user content. Customer review sites like Yelp, TripAdvisor, FlyerTalk, and FatWallet are all Web sites where the business is only about enlisting the end user to create its value. YouTube, the video sharing site, provides no products. It is a Web service that lets you post and view videos posted by other users. Because videos take a lot of bandwidth (that is, they need to be served by large computers), you can't post and view videos from just any Web site. YouTube created huge value for itself, not by selling or creating anything, but by providing a service that anyone can use and that anyone can access. The end users, people who post their videos to YouTube's site, are the people who are adding value. The visitors, the people who view videos, are why YouTube is worth so much.

User-generated content needs to be properly managed. Managers of these sites need to keep close track of the content placed on the sites so that they accumulate undesirable material. For example, YouTube constantly has to ensure that it is not redistributing copyrighted material. Similarly, the user comment sites need to be monitored to ensure that the commentaries do not diverge into other topics that may be vulgar, controversial, or subversive (unless their intention is to provide a forum for these).

4.6 "Intel Inside"

Most people, when they buy a PC, have no idea of the technology used inside it. Intel is one of the major manufacturers of the chips that drive PCs, and "Intel Inside" is the way Intel has branded itself to the general market. Intel decided that it was important for people to understand that their chips were running PCs and created a large marketing campaign to brand their technology. They worked with PC makers to include a label on the outside of computers, highlighting that their chip was being used inside them. The goal was to create name recognition for an enabling technology, which is a technology that makes things work but is not seen by the end user. Most companies believe that brand recognition helps their company compete in the marketplace. They believe that, if people view their brand as being superior, they will then specify the brand, even if they are unaware of the brand's function or are not directly buying their service.

On the Web, a lot of products are not directly accessed by the end user but are used to power Web sites and Web applications. With the growth of mashups, technologies that are a core component for—that is, are behind—a new service are not directly accessed and thus not necessarily known to the people using the service. The company that owns the core service wants brand recognition. Google provides a core service with Google Earth, which is a photomapping of the earth. The satellite images available from Google Earth may be used by many different services, such as environmental groups like Appalachian Voices (iLoveMountains.org), a nonprofit that campaigns against the removal of mountaintops for coal mining. Appalachian Voices has created an application to show Americans how their power use is connected to mountaintop removal. Visitors who type in their zip code are taken to a map of the United States, which shows the connection between the visitor's electric use and the plants that produce the power to the coal mines that harvest energy. The Appalachian Voices Web site has layered on top of Google Earth icons that represent power plants and mines. Visitors can zoom in to see a satellite image of a removed mountain top. The map is branded by Google Earth even though visitors do not go to the Google site or realize that they are actively using a Google service. Because the underlying service is theirs, Google wants to make sure visitors are aware of their connection.

4.7 Providing Services Above the Level of a Single Device

As the computer industry matures, technologies converge. Convergence, the bringing together of technologies, results in wider availability of new applications on a greater number of platforms. In the 1980s, IBM decoupled the operating system of the PC from the hardware. In the 1990s, the browser decoupled the application from the computer. Currently, browsers are allowing applications to be decoupled from the computer, thereby allowing applications to become available above the level of any single device. This development provides end users with the ability to access applications from whatever device they are on, be that a computer, a personal digital assistant (PDA), or a cell phone. In theory the technology is available today. In practice, Web designers and their managers need to understand the ramifications of developing applications above the single device: The capabilities of the browser become more important than the capabilities of the computer device hosting the browser.

Correctly designed Web pages can be accessed by any device. For that to happen, the Web designer must be aware of the technical and technological requirements of design, such as

- Scalability.
- Format specifications.
- Browsers.
- Viewing devices.

Scalability

The Web is an elegantly designed technology because it is both simple and scalable. Its ability to scale and support thousands, millions, and even billions of people and transactions highlights the elegance of its design. Web technologies, when used correctly, allow Web sites to harness this scalability.

The challenge is that most designers come from the print world and that they are used to designing for an 8.5 × 11-inch (or A4) sheet of paper. They like the control that comes from being able to specify the minute placement of objects on a page. Whereas the output of a printed page is a fixed size piece of paper, the output of a Web page is a browser whose size is unknown ahead of time. The Web is not a printer: Specifying a Web page's design absolutely, so that each element's placement is precisely specified, hinders the use of the page. During the creation of a Web page, the creator has no idea of the size of the end user's screen, the resolution of the screen, or the size of the browser within the screen. By building a site specifying that the page is 800×600 pixels, the designer marginalizes most of the people on the Web. On a high-resolution screen, the page appears as an itty-bitty page using a quarter of the screen. Meanwhile, the page is completely inaccessible by people using cell phones or PDAs because it overflows the screen. The goal of any Web site is to allow access, not to repel visitors. (See Figure 4.2.)

Format Specifications

In the design of a Web page, the page implementation must be based on W3C (World Wide Web Consortium) standards. The people at

Figure 4.2 Web Page on a cell phone and computer monitor.

W3C invented the Web and control the documents specifying the acceptable formats for pages. The W3C's goal is to ensure that the Web is accessible by as many devices as possible under as many circumstances as possible. To maintain this accessibility, the W3C sets standards. A couple of the standards they set are:

1. HyperText Markup Language (HTML), the scripting language of the Web.
2. Cascading Style Sheets (CSS), the design and layout language of the Web.

Designers who want to make sure that their content is accessible by any device need to follow the W3C standards. Using W3C recommendations for creating a Web page assures designers that people entering the site on different devices with different resolutions and screen sizes can actually view the Web site and have similar experiences.

Browsers

Web browsers do not all work the same. Currently, the major browsers are MS Internet Explorer and Mozilla Firefox. Mozilla Firefox follows the W3C standards more closely than MS Internet Explorer, which follows only the standards that Microsoft finds useful for business purposes; Microsoft feels it must implement some standards, and it chooses to ignore or replace others with their own definitions.

In addition, every release of MS Internet Explorer behaves differently with respect to certain aspects of the standards like style sheets. For example, MS Internet Explorer Version 6 Service Pack 2 (Explorer 6.2) does not support multimedia unless the file is in the same directory as the HTML file. However, multimedia files tend to be large, and most organizations prefer to store all their large files in a central directory on the server. Explorer's 6.2 implementation is different from all other browsers that support links to multimedia. The effect is that every time Microsoft releases a new version of their browser, Web designers need to make sure their sites still work with the new release.

Viewing Devices

More than a minor inconvenience are the technical limitations of smartphones, cell phones, and PDAs that include browsers. Currently about 10 percent of the cell phones in America are smartphones. Within the next eight years, that percentage will grow to about half the phones. Each smartphone vendor has its own browser, and each browser has its own limitations. Designers have to understand the technical limitations of the different devices accessing their Web pages. Accessing applications from PDAs and cell phones is an issue that needs to be thought through before designing a site. Because of their small screen size and the lack of homogeneity, designers cannot design intuitively for cell phones and PDAs. Of all the different PDA and cell phones on the market, each browser supports a different subset of capabilities and plug-ins. For example, as of 2008, none of these browsers support plug-ins like Flash or Java (another language for interactive Web-based applications). Most of the browsers do not support JavaScript, a local programming language that allows simple interactivity like grading simple test questions. And filling out forms on Web pages can be very difficult because of the unique behavior of some of the browsers.

The main smartphone operating systems (and browsers) are:

- Nokia's Symbian.
- Portable versions of Linux.
- MS Windows.
- Mozilla's Minimo.
- Palm's Garnet.

As of 2007, according to Gartner Group, Symbian had 70 percent of the mobile OS market, and Linux had 15 percent. Of the balance, RIM's Blackberry had 5 percent and Microsoft Windows 5 percent.

Web site designers who want to access the mobile marketplace need to understand the differences and build content that these devices can easily access. For example, in Windows Mobile you can't use JavaScript, Flash, or style sheets. Zooming and frames are poor. Meanwhile, Symbian and Minimo support most standard browser functions and handle zooming and frames well. Alternatively, Apple's iPhone browser works well though it supports only Apple plug-ins; so it has no Flash support, and video or multimedia is not visible.

4.8 Social Networking

A Web phenomenon not mentioned back in 2004 (because it was still in its infancy and not yet important), when "Web 2.0" was coined, is social networking. Social networking has been around on the Web since the 1990s. In the last few years, however, social networking has taken off. The most notable social networking sites are MySpace and Facebook, sites that provide the infrastructure for people to create and share their biographical information.

Social networking consists of services that allow members to create personal profiles, where they can blog about their daily activities, share information of interest to them, and share pictures and movies. People with social networking sites let others have access to this information, or, in social networking terms, they share their information with friends. The control of what friends can view of your content has created its own subculture. Social networking sites allow members to invite friends, who must then accept the invitation, thereby creating a two-way acceptance. Many social networking members like to brag about the number of friends they have, although, after many degrees of friendship, the word "friend" is only loosely applicable.

This large network of loosely connected friendships can be very entertaining, but it also may create security issues. Predators can easily worm their way into one "friend's" site and use it as a jumping off platform to access many other friends' sites. Young people who do not yet understand the ramifications of overexposure may inadvertently provide too much information to potentially the wrong audience. The biggest issue to consider for social networking is the change in culture that these networks enable. Young people of today find it compelling to share intimate and personal experiences on their pages. This information could be come problematic in the future. For example, if a comment about a business supervisor came to the attention of the boss, there could be consequences on the job, or a potential boss might not so inclined to hire the source of the comment.

Networking in the Business World

Social networking is different for businesses than for individuals. Acceptance is much slower and much more cautious among business organizations. Some companies have used social networking infrastructures as a way to allow employees better access to each other. The mind-set of social networking sites within a corporate environment is very different from that found on MySpace and Facebook, which are in a public, individual-based environment.

For example, IBM has used social networks as a human resources service. Employees can fill out a page about themselves, state the projects they are working on currently and in the past, and identify their chain of command; they can also share hobbies and passions. Other employees can access these pages to learn about each other. Connecting with one another aids employees on a professional and personnel level and in finding out about opportunities within the company. This kind of network is helpful in any organization that spans the world. Employees may need to work with someone on a different continent and need to have an idea of the person's background.

Networking Among Adults

In the living, breathing, continuously changing page found on consumer social networking sites, acceptance among adults, as in the business world, is restrained and cautious. The difference may be because adults, especially those with children, don't have the spare time to frequently update a social networking page, are less interested in the daily minutia of others, and are concerned about privacy. They do not feel comfortable with their identity and personal details being available to the general public.

From an adult point of view, social networking is a good way keep in touch with friends and colleagues from previous schools and jobs, but the type of information shared is typically relatively reserved and factual. Adoption is slow due to lack of a critical mass. If none of your friends are networking socially, there is little impetus to start. Even well connected, technically savvy adults are slow to use these sites. Most adults, when asked why they are not social networking, mention relevance, privacy concerns, and time: How much time should I spend updating my information? What benefit will this provide? How much access do I want to give other people to my private or work life?

Wikis

Most adults would be interested in a social network simply to maintain contact with like-minded folks and to keep up-to-date. In many situations, a wiki (a collaborative encyclopedia) may be a better fit for businesses and adults. On the Web, Wikipedia is a great source of information on many popular and obscure subjects.

Most businesspeople are less interested in finding out the details of other people's personal life and more interested in finding out the details of products, services, and issues. Within a company, a wiki can be used in a number of ways, for example, to provide a repository with up-to-the-minute information or technical documentation on products.

- Customers can be given access to wiki-based documentation that is continually being updated. Because everyone can update and add to a wiki, customers who find the documentation lacking can comment on incomplete instructions or provide suggestions to other customers about an easier way to use a feature.

- Wikis can also be used within a company as a collective document. Members of an internal team who are creating a new product can add comments on new features or update the status of features in development.

- Professional organizations can use wikis to harness their collective knowledge. Specialists in a field can create and add to a wiki, creating a living document that can be used to move the field ahead.

These new applications being developed based on existing Web technologies are permitting the general user community greater access to content for the Web. In addition, they are providing new services and ever more information by combining data from multiple sources, and they are changing the distribution of the infrastructure of where end users process their data and documents.

4.9 Checklist

__ Questions to ask before creating documents that reside on someone else's hard drive are:
1. Will the company sell my data?
2. Will they hand it over to a government if that government asks?
3. How long will they store the data?
4. Who else has access to the data?
5. Will they use my private data to sell me other services?
6. Do I have to keep paying them so that that they don't delete it?

__ Before relying on applications services, consider the environment. Questions to ask are:
1. How accessible is the application during travel?
2. Does it work well even with poor or spotty Internet service?

5.0

Web 2.0 Technologies

Technology trends and capabilities are all possible because new capabilities are developed on top of existing infrastructures or because new infrastructures mature. This chapter provides a nontechnical explanation of the latest Web 2.0 technologies and their implications, so that managers can understand their benefits as well as where they can be used.

 By the end of this chapter, you should be able to:

- Identify the latest Web 2.0 technologies.
- Explain Rich Site Summary (RSS).
- Describe podcasts.
- Describe Web techniques.
- Identify the uses of HTML and XML.
- Understand Web 3.0.

5.1 Web 2.0 Technologies

It is important for people who are not working in information technology (IT) to understand the technologies being talked about in today's market. SMEs, business managers, and trainers need to talk to their IT departments and sit in on vendor sessions as they embrace e-learning. It is very easy to get hoodwinked, overwhelmed, or sold unnecessary or nonfunctional solutions if you don't understand the basics of the technologies being discussed. This chapter provides you with enough understanding so that you can listen to a technical conversation given by an IT person or a salesperson and be able to separate reality from hyperbole. By the end of the chapter you should have enough information to follow a technical conversation, ask intelligent questions, and feel comfortable listening to the presentation.

The technologies that discussed in this chapter are

- Rich site summary (RSS).
- Podcasts.
- Web Techniques.
- HTML and XML.

5.2 Rich Site Summary (RSS)

RSS (rich site summary) is a simple service that has enabled Web 2.0 functionality. RSS is a broadcast tool that could also be called a digital feed, a mechanism that is used to send digital content using the Internet. What makes RSS so useful is that you can set it up to send out a message when a change is made to existing content. Content providers can add RSS capabilities to their Web blog or Web site. Every time they change their blog or site, a message is sent to the service subscribers. The advantage to subscribers is that they do not have to actively return to the site to look for updates; they receive notifications of the updates when they occur. (The RSS is the actual feed or message that is sent out.) So if you like a site or a blog that provides an RSS feed, you can register and then just check your e-mail to find out about changes and updates.

This service is the most prevalent on blogging sites. If you subscribe, every time the blogger updates the blog, you are notified. This feature works especially well for people who follow blogging sites that are not updated on a published schedule or that are irregularly changed.

Businesses can use this type of service to better inform customers on the status of an order. A business can connect their manufacturing or delivery system to their customers through an RSS feed. Instead of obliging the customer to visit a Web site for the status of a purchase or delivery, the system can automatically send a message about status changes.

Delivery providers like FedEx and United Parcel Service offer this service to their customers. When a vendor ships an order through one of these delivery providers, e-mails detailing the current location of the product are sent to the end customers as the package makes its way through the delivery system. This service benefits both the customer and the provider: The customer has up-to-date knowledge of supply location, and the provider reduces its support costs to handle shipment inquiries from end customers.

RSS can also be helpful for merchant services. For example, a merchant that sells antique toys on its Web site can use RSS. When the merchant updates the catalog, a message can be sent to any collectors who subscribe to the RSS feed. Collectors might sign up for RSS feeds from multiple antique toy merchants located across the country or around the world. They no longer need to troll the merchants' sites looking for new products. They can wait to be notified when something new is posted and then purchase what meets their needs.

RSS service is particularly popular on social networking sites. People who like to read other peoples' social networking pages want to be notified when those pages change. With RSS they don't need to revisit the pages to see whether changes were made. Subscribers to the page are notified when there is new content.

This kind of technology can be easily translated to e-learning, where users can sign up for updates to courses in which they are particularly interested or that they can use for references purposes after taking a traditional training course.

5.3 Podcasts

With the Internet, everything old is new again. Podcasts are a perfect example. Do you remember the Sony Walkman™? When the Walkman first appeared, we could go jogging with our music, bringing the music with us when we traveled. The portable format let us listen to our music when we wanted to and where we wanted to, without disturbing anyone else. What wasn't so convenient was the bag of cassette tapes we needed to carry wherever we went. What is nice about *podcasting* is that, with the large disk space available today, you can download all your music to your digital player and listen to your choices of music without having to cart around anything other then the player.

The word "podcast" came about from splicing together the two words: "iPod" and "broadcast." Technically speaking, podcasts are digital media files compressed. The podcast portion relates to being able to download the audio file from a Web site. RSS can be used in conjunction with a podcast, allowing users to subscribe to a podcast service. Users can either be notified when new content becomes available or have the new content automatically downloaded to their PC or digital media player.

Podcasts are popular because of the portability and flexibility they offer. Any audio or video can be saved in a format that can be podcasted—that is, streamed to a PC or downloaded onto a portable player. This has freed end users from having to take a collection of tapes or CDs with them. Content creators no longer need to publish their material onto physical media like cassette tapes or compact discs. From a technological point of view, this is a very small change, but it is huge in that it cuts out the need for the creation and distribution of physical media. (Production and content development steps have not changed.) This one small technological step has resulted in a major economic upheaval for the recording industry.

Freed from physical media, people now have many more choices. Web sites can serve the Long Tail of users by breaking albums into individual songs and providing access to new or niche artists. Unestablished musicians and radio personalities can record themselves and save these recordings as podcasts. The elimination of the need for physical media provides direct access to potential customers and cuts out the costs and hassles of physical distribution. This development has had devastating consequences for traditional media. Large record stores like Tower Records have gone out of business because of the competition, and the record industry as a whole is still coming to terms with the effects of the Internet.

This upheaval and the related loss of revenue have two basic causes:

1. Disintermediation, whereby customers can purchase content directly from the artists rather than through established distribution channels.

2. The ease of duplication of digital content—and downloading a copy of the audio file is in essence duplication. Once content is digital, it is harder for companies to charge and control the copies of it.

On the whole, however, organizations have benefited from podcasting. Traditionally, when an organization wanted to create an audio recording, it incurred a high cost of reproduction and distribution. That cost has gone away.

Although podcasts can add new life to e-learning, providing creators with an audio capability they might not otherwise have, designers must remember that a song does not get better when played on an iPod as opposed to being played on a Walkman. In an e-learning course, if a learner is listening to an engaging (or boring) narration, it is equally engaging (or boring) whether it is played on a Walkman or delivered as a podcast. Several years ago, for example, I needed to listen to a series of corporate presentations delivered on cassette tapes and decided to use my commute to listen to them. However, I soon realized that, having arrived at work, I couldn't remember a thing the narrator had said. The effect could not have been any different if I'd downloaded the audio track from a podcast and played it on a digital audio player in the car today.

5.4 Web Techniques

New Web techniques are enabling the changes we see and learn about on the Web. Three areas in play for any Web application: the browser, the network, and the server (see Figure 5.1).

Web browsers are stateless, that is, they have no memory. Browsers can talk to the network and display what the network sends to them, but they can't really remember what was displayed or what actions the reader took. Servers have all the memory. Initially this was a fine paradigm. People created HTML pages that were displayed over the Web through a browser. Eventually, however, content developers dreamed up more interesting applications, and new techniques and delivery mechanisms were needed to actualize these applications.

To get browsers to do more then just display a page, technologies like JavaScript, VBScript, Java, and ActionScript (Flash)

Figure 5.1 Web technologies.

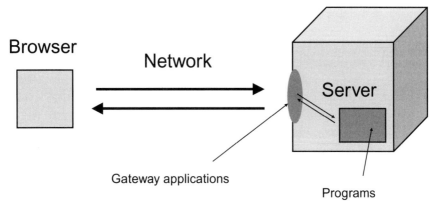

were created. These helper applications, or scripts, have several functions:

- They take information passed to them and display it in the browser.
- They can parse information, that is, they can split up, separate, and figure out what to do with the data sent to the browser.
- They support the ability to redraw a small piece of the page without having to reload the entire page.

To support these new functionalities, browsers needed to be updated to Netscape 6 or later, to Firefox 1.0 or later, and to Internet Explorer 5.5. In the case of helper applications like Java and Macromedia Flash, additional software maybe needed on the reader's computer. However, the plug-in can greatly enhance the browser's capability. For example, video players like QuickTime or Windows Media Player allow movies to be shown from a browser.

The big advances have come primarily from plug-ins like Java and Flash, which now can be used to program entire interactive environments, enabling end users to:

- See motion.
- Input WYSIWYG content.
- Have almost real-time interactivity.
- Transmit and receive data from the servers.

Such capability has led to, for example, the creation of entire Office application suites (word processing, spreadsheet, e-mail client) where the content is hosted on the server but the interface is presented in the browser.

On the server side, two types of technologies are employed.

1. Technologies that connect the network to the application.
2. The actual applications.

Technologies like Common Gateway Interface (CGI), Active Server Pages (ASP), ColdFusion, and Java 2 Enterprise Edition (J2EE) are the connecting technologies. They connect to the network and send information to and from applications. For example, when you fill out a form on a Web page, the browser transmits your input through the network. The connector technology (e.g., CGI) receives the data packet from the browser and passes it to an application. The application:

- Reads the packet.
- Breaks it down into individual pieces.
- Figures out what to do with the data.
- Process and/or stores it.
- Prepares a reply packet to send back to your browser through the connecting technology and the network.

Applications have been around since the dawn of computers. Application developer use the computer language they think provides them with the functionality they need. Each language has a set of libraries or prewritten functions that facilitate creating new applications.

- Business applications have traditionally been written in COBOL.
- Engineering applications have been traditionally written in FORTRAN.
- Many other applications are written in C or C++.

Web developers have created a new set of languages to help them create Web applications. Among the new languages are Perl, PHP, and TCL (pronounced tickle). These languages are good at processing text, and they don't need to be compiled. They are fast to write, but they run more slowly than traditional languages, and debugging them is harder.

As the Internet evolves, more functionality is needed at the level of the browser. To support this additional functionality, new methods are created and browsers are updated. One of the most recent updates is called AJAX (asynchronous JavaScript and XML). AJAX allows the browser and server to interact more flexibly than before so that there is interactivity in the client's browser. It is available in browsers newer than Netscape 7, Firefox 1.0 and Internet Explorer 6.2. Before AJAX, when a browser form was filled out and transmitted to a Web server for processing, the Web server responded with a completely new page, which replaced the previous page that the browser was displaying. With AJAX and the updated browsers, the server no longer needs to replace the whole page. A small portion of it can be changed locally when the response is received from the server.

An application like Google Docs, for example, uses AJAX. When using Google Docs' Document program, AJAX allows the transmission of the current document contents, as input by the user, without having to replace and redraw the whole page being viewed. In essence, as the author types in keystrokes, AJAX can transmit them to the server for storage.

The downside to the increased browser functionality (from plug-ins like Flash, Media Player, and the like) is that there are more security concerns. When the browser could display only a page of content, the security threat to a client's computer from Web applications was small. With the plug-ins providing more connection between the client's computer and the Internet, damage can be done to the client's privacy or data through more channels. The more intelligence there is on a browser, the more it is necessary to keep an eye on the browser and plug-in security settings.

5.5 HyperText Markup Language (HTML) and Extensible Markup Language (XML)

HyperText Markup Language (HTML)

HTML (HyperText Markup Language) is the information display language that powered the Internet's rise. It is commonly used to create Web pages and has helped make e-learning courses more pleasant to look at and navigate—and ultimately more effective. HTML is a simple set of formatting instructions so that text can be positioned and displayed as if it were being produced from a high-quality printer. Because of its simplicity and power, it is easily learned and has been widely adopted.

In the early years of the Web, the formatting of Web pages was done in-line. That means if you wanted a title to be bold, an HTML programmer would put a tag before the words for the title and an end tag after the title telling the browser to bold the text between the tags. This worked well but was not very flexible. To change the titles on 1,000 pages, someone had to physically change each page. To solve this dilemma, W3C came up with Cascading Style Sheets (CSS). Previous HTML tags were still supported but new CSS tags could be used to define formatting. With CSS, the formatting instructions can be placed in a central, separate file that can be shared by multiple Web pages. For example, a label called title can be created. Instead of defining attributes like bold, font size, and color for every instance of the title text, a developer can simply mark the text as being a title. In the CSS file, the developer then defines the display attributes for that title tag. To change all the text tagged as title, a Web designer goes to a CSS page and changes the attributes for title; all the Web pages using that style sheet file then display the new formatting. Separating the appearance from the textual content provided greater design flexibility and easier Web site maintenance.

Web developers looked at how easy HTML made it to publish formatted information and thought that this could also be used to share data. Storage formats like Microsoft Excel's .xls or Microsoft Word's .doc are specific to a computer system and an application; they cannot be shared easily with other computer systems or applications. A text-based storage format improves the transportability of data.

Extensible Markup Language (XML)

W3C created XML (Extensible Markup Language) as an extended version of HTML with features for data storage. XML has a double role:

1. It can act as a display language: Web pages built in XML can be displayed in a formatted manner, just as in HTML.

2. It can be used as a structured data storage format. Instead of storing a database in binary machine- and application-dependent format, the data can be stored in XML.

Like HTML, XML uses tags, which define the data. For example, a tag like First_Name can be used to store the first name of an employee. To make the data usable, a parser (an application that can read in the data and break it up into usable chunks) needs to be deployed. For example, a parser can take an XML document with a list of employees that includes the courses they have taken and create tables associating employee names with the course names. The tables can then be sorted, printed, and used for other purposes.

XML supports the nesting of data. As an example, if you have one structure with employee courses, another structure with employee benefits, and a third with employee contact information, you can create a fourth structure that includes all of these for a particular employee. The fourth structure can be replicated for each employ. This ability to bridge multiple structures is what databases do. Since XML is text based (machine independent), it can be used as the basic format to store and transmit structured data sets over the Web.

The caveat with XML is that someone needs to create intelligence, that is, a program that will interpret what is being read. That is, when an XML page is received, something at the user end needs to know what each field means and what needs to be done with it. Many vendors tout that their systems use XML, but you need to ask the next question: What data definition is the vendor using? If the vendor is using their own data definitions, you know they are using a Web methodology but their solution is still proprietary. Therefore it might not be readily reusable.

To reuse different data definitions, a programmer needs to create a filter. For example, two different departments in an organization may use XML to create data structures for the information they are saving. Somewhere along the line, they want to share these structures. Because these are different data structures, the probability is high that they will encounter a number of problems. For example:

- They probably named their fields differently. For example, they may have defined the field for the employee's first name differently. One department may have used "fname," and the second department used "First_Name."
- Two fields in different data structures may have the same tag name, but each department defined the field differently. Both structures could have a field named value, but in one structure value is defined as product cost, whereas the other structure defines value as the retail price.

To translate between two different XML structures, a programmer can use XSLT, a programming language that reformats XML but needs to know the definition of each field in each structure before reformatting them.

XSLT can also be used to translate a given XML format into a different format for display. So, if you created a data set using XML, you can use XSLT to translate it into PDF (portable document format), MS Word, or Docbook XML. You can also display an XML page using XSL (Extensible Style Sheet Language) is the display format for XML pages, analogous to CSS for HTML.

A security caveat: Be careful about storing proprietary data on your Web server in a Web-browsable area, which is a set of folders that can be reached by end users using just their browser. Typically, Web pages are published in this area. Because XML can now be used as a Web page display language, many developers are placing their XML data in browsable areas. However, proprietary data that you want to share should *not* be put in a Web browse-able area. Instead, an application (like a relational database or a Web form processor) should serve the XML-format data based on the user requests; such a program can be used to authenticate users to ensure that the data (in its raw form) does not get into the wrong hands.

5.6 Web 3.0

No one knows what the Web will look like in 10 years. Nor do we know what social phenomena will push the Web in a new direction. The best we can do today, when we want to look into the future, is to look at the future technologies under discussion and extrapolate the applications that these technologies might support.

Today's technology leaders are talking about the benefit of higher-bandwidth networks and device-independent access, both of which are just extensions of current solutions. The biggest technological leap under discussion today is the Semantic Web. The Semantic Web is championed by Tim Berners-Lee, the inventor of the World Wide Web. The idea behind it is a merger of data, information, and knowledge exchange. The sci-fi theory behind Semantic Web is that it will allow computers to do the tedious work that humans have to do, enabling artificial intelligence—all done by turning the Web into one big database.

To understand the theory behind the Semantic Web, look at what databases are currently doing for us. Back in the 1950s, if a company had 10,000 employees, all the employees' files sat in paper file folders in a big file cabinet. To update an employee's training information, a manager had either to send the training piece of paper to Human Resources (HR) to be placed in that employee's personnel file or to create his or her own training files, separate from the file sitting in Human Resources. If the employee moved to a different department, someone from HR had to manually change the file and physically hand it to the new manager. The old manager would need then to remember to give any of other files on that employee to the new manager.

With a computer-based database, all employee information is stored electronically. Through the database software, each manager has access to a different view or portion of the data. HR may have access to benefits-related information, training may have access to education-related records, and the employee's manager may have access to performance history. With all information residing centrally, a training manager, with proper access, could create a report to compare performance history to training completion. However powerful a database, each employee is limited to searching only the data that resides within that database. With a database, when an worker transfers from one department to another, allowing the new manager to access the file may involve just changing the access permissions on the employee's records.

With the Semantic Web, all data on the Web becomes an XML-based portion of a much larger database. Anyone on the Web can collect data from multiple XML files to expand the scope of an application. For example, a real estate company may be saving in their database the history of house prices in a particular neighborhood. Meanwhile, the local city government may be saving the history of road improvements in its database. Without something like the Semantic Web, to find out how road improvements affected the prices of houses, an organization could:

- Get a copy of each databases to perform a search.
- Merge the database by translating and loading one database into the other.
- Carry out their inquiry only once all the data is merged into a single database.

The semantic Web's goal is to eliminate the need to merge separate databases provided over the Web. In our example, the data from the town and from the real estate company would be openly available for users to merge so that they could create new applications. In theory, this is a next generation of mashups (Chapter 4.0). Currently, mashups pull data from multiple Web page sources, but merging them is not easy. A highly skilled programmer needs to read each set of the data's API (Application Programming Interfaces), create filters, and write programs to redisplay the information. With the Semantic Web, all the data on the Web would be in XML, so that it can be categorized, accessed, and reformatted easily to provide new applications and services.

6.0

Web 2.0 Trends for e-Learning

As we have learned, e-learning is a subset of the Web. All trends, technologies, and services that are found on the Web can be applied to e-learning. In Chapter 4.0, we looked at some of the trends and technologies of Web 2.0 in general. In this chapter, we'll look at how some of those same trends and technologies are applied specifically to e-learning courses. This discussion should help managers understand the benefits and limitations of each trend and technology as they apply specifically to e-learning.

 By the end of this chapter, you should be able to:

- Identify how Web trends are applied to e-learning 2.0.
- Describe how application services are applied to e-learning 2.0.
- Understand how the Long Tail applies to e-learning 2.0.
- Explain how to enlist end users to add value.

- Understand microcontent.
- Describe how to furnish services beyond the PC.
- Show how "Intel Inside" applies to e-learning 2.0.
- Understand new technologies and how they relate to e-learning 2.0.
- Identify what a 2.0 e-learning course looks like.

6.1 Web Trends and e-Learning 2.0

We need to know how the Web 2.0 trends and technologies are applied to e-learning, where the end user is the learner, and the supplier is the course creator, trainer, or training organization. Further, companies that provide learning management systems (LMSs), authoring tools, and simulation tools are the enabling technologies used by trainers to provide 2.0 services to end users. Learning management systems, authoring tools, and simulation tools are to trainers what a database is to Google: the behind-the-scenes engine to provide the service.

If not all fashions are for everyone, then not all technologies are for everyone. Even though a technology is in fashion, it does not have to be deployed. The goal is to provide effective, accessible learning, not to show off that you can use a new technology.

• • • • • • • • • • •

Case Study: Knowledge Pills

Knowledge Pills, Inc., is a Web 2.0 e-learning company that develops short, 15-minute training courses for the corporate marketplace. Knowledge Pills's goal is to provide companies with employee-directed courses that can be taken just-in-time throughout the business cycle. Daniel Purlich, CEO of Knowledge Pills, sees his company as a knowledge provider: "Like most people who access an application service, visitors to our site or clients that put our products on their intranet do not want their end users to feel like they are accessing technology." Employees should be able to search a string of words in their corporate search engine, and a Knowledge Pill containing this information should come up. Employees can take a course on whatever device they use without restrictions or needing additional technology that will slow them down.

One of the first courses that Knowledge Pills built was "Doing Business in China." There are 450-page books and weeklong seminars on doing business in China for the manager who is moving to China to run an operation. Managers who are flying to China for a two-day business trip do not have the desire for this breadth and depth of information. They want a 15-minute course that highlights basic courtesies and business etiquette. This type of quick-to-take course—focused on Long Tail subjects and of interest to a small specific market—is what Knowledge Pills provides. Knowledge Pills has a course catalog of short courses on hundreds of subjects that help workers stay in tune with and up-to-date on current issues, trends, and technologies that affect them on a daily basis.

Knowledge Pills has also shaken up the traditional sales model. Purlich has been pitching courses for over 20 years. "I was always frustrated that the course was missing in the sales pitch," says Purlich. "Few purchasers of training courses ever take an entire course they purchase; many times they buy courses without ever seeing them. We embrace the modern concept that information should be accessible. With Knowledge Pills, wide samplings of the training courses we offer are available on the web site. You don't need special passwords to access the training and you can take an entire training course, not just a couple pages that show how pretty the training looks." Purlich also believes in enlisting the end user to add value to the training process, wikis, newsgroups, student comments, and rankings should be part of any training course. Knowledge Pills courses are initially available in four languages (English, French, Spanish, and German), and eventually they will be provided in many more languages. The Knowledge Pills philosophy is that learners should be able to take courses in the language they are most comfortable with.

Many of Knowledge Pills ideas about the type, length, and accessibility of e-learning come from founder Daniel Purlich's experience in the training marketplace. Purlich comes from a traditional training and e-learning background. In the 1990 he was the general manager of France Telecom's training division, where he was responsible for identifying corporate training direction, purchasing, and developing initially computer-based training (CBT) training and eventually e-learning courses. More recently, Purlich was director of content development at Educaterra, the training arm of Telefonica, the second largest telecommunications company in the world. In 2004, his organization at Educaterra provided 90,000 Telefonica employees with over a million hours of training a year.

Purlich worked closely with managers throughout Telefonica to understand their needs and requirements. What became quickly apparent was a fundamental change in training that managers were requesting. Managers did not want to take their employees out of the workplace for training, yet changes in technology and business operations were happening frequently and quickly. Although managers needed to be assured that employees were up-to-date on these changes, they could not afford to have employees out of the office for days at a time. What managers wanted were brief, 15-minute, training sessions that employees could take anywhere, when the need arose, and that provided the nuggets of information they needed to perform their jobs or participate effectively in a meeting or conference call.

Purlich realized that, for his organization to react to this change, they needed to change the size and scope of course production. Courses needed to be reorganized and prioritized differently. The company needed many cheap-to-produce, short training courses on subjects that were pertinent today but may not be pertinent in the future. These courses had to work on any resolution monitor, PDA, or cell phone. Managers throughout the organization were happy with the direction training was heading, even as they realized that classroom training and traditional e-learning would not go away. Quick, cheap, rapid e-learning courses provided them with the necessary training infrastructure that employees need to do their job now. Purlich found that these courses were very popular with employees because they allowed them to keep up with trends and their workload.

• • • • • • • • • • • •

6.2 Application Services

End users can use some applications without having to run anything on their computer (as discussed earlier in the book): These are application services. For example, using a mapping application that helps us with directions, visitors only have to enter the Web site and put in their starting-from and going-to addresses, and a map with directions appears. Visitors do not have to download anything; they are unaware of the software running behind the scenes. All they are aware of is the user interface and the results—the information being displayed.

In the context of e-learning, courses are the application service. Learners enter a training site or Web course, take the course, complete the tests, and are done. They do not need to download software or learn a new application. They are completely unaware of any behind-the-scene technology. Like all effective application services, an effective e-learning course has only to adhere to a couple of the principles and practices of good Web design:

- All pages should display quickly without the need of a plug-in.
- Appropriate local and global navigation should be used, navigation that allows the learner to move between pages and that provides easy access to course-wide features like help, glossary, FAQ, and a site map.

The learner should never be aware of any integration with other systems like an LMS. From the learner's point of view, all aspects of a course should work transparently.

6.3 The Long Tail

In e-learning, the Long Tail consists of either learners who don't fall into the training department's core market or traditionally hard-to-reach learners. (See Chapter 4.0 for how the Long Tail applies to Web 2.0 technology.) Many courses in today's organization are

Long Tail courses; that is, they are applicable to only a small number of employees or available to employees who find it difficult to attend a course given at a specific time, on a specific day, at the organization's headquarters.

Many organizations have employees working outside the office, and pulling them out of the field is not easy. When it is necessary to pull these employees out of the field, the organization typically optimizes their time by offering multiple courses over one to a few days. When planning the curriculum for these sessions, training managers look at all the training they could possibly provide the employees, prioritize the courses, and present only a subset of the total. As a result, due to time constraints, many subjects are never presented.

Turning training into Web courses is another way to reach these hard-to-reach learners. Training over the Web does not negate the need to pull employees out of the field or to provide classroom training, but it does give organizations access to employees who are not easily available. Instead of cramming all the training into a one to a few days at a centralized session, management can decide which training works best as e-learning and which works best in a classroom. They can then optimize the classroom sessions and provide the other sessions as e-learning.

What many organizations find is that product training, services training, and certification training work well as e-learning—a series of rapid e-learning courses on products, services, and certification requirements. In particular, some of these courses may be of interest to only a small percentage of field employees; these are called niche courses. With classroom training, a niche course is typically given infrequently. When the course is available as e-learning, employees can take it when they need it, not having to wait until the next time it is offered.

. . . .

Case Study: Devereux

Devereux is a nonprofit organization providing services around the United States for persons with emotional, developmental, and educational disabilities. Devereux also provides products and consulting services to assist other child welfare, mental health, and special education organizations. Devereux has 18 centers with over 6,000 employees who support over 15,000 individuals and families with special needs.

Certification and licensing are recurring mandatory requirements for all of Devereux's employees and hundreds of contractors. Most of Devereux's clinical staffers work in nontraditional workplaces like client homes. They do not have fixed lunch periods or breaks, and typically they work far from Devereux's offices. Employees are responsible for a wide variety of tasks. They are often in more than one location on a given day. For all these reasons, pulling them out of the field to provide training and testing is logistically complicated and time-consuming.

Yet Devereux's training department management had to contend with the difficulties of scheduling training for the 18 offices spread throughout the United States without losing trainers to exhaustion and burnout. They wanted to provide training that met the needs of the learners and their managers. What they wanted was training when and where it was convenient to them.

Mary Imbornone, Devereux's national director of training, believed that e-learning was an answer to many of Devereux's logistical issues. Initially Mary bought an off-the-shelf suite of courses, which she found expensive and too generic to meet the needs of Devereux's specific population. Mary decided to bring e-learning in-house and create training that specifically met the needs of the employees.

Devereux hired an e-learning training specialist to create a two-day boot camp for all 18 people in their training department, none of whom had ever been involved in e-learning. Most of the boot camp was spent teaching the fundamental tactics of effectively moving training to the Web. Additionally, Devereux set up a council where they laid out company-wide standards and practices for e-learning courses. To simplify and focus e-learning development, Devereux split trainers into three different groups based on the types of training needed by the employees. They then created a suite of courses that were available to all field workers.

Feedback from the field was very positive. Employees stated that they appreciated that they could receive self-paced training and that Devereux was no longer forcing them to attend live sessions. Both the employees and consultants were able to receive certification training when it was convenient for them. Devereux's e-learning site has received lots of activity. According to Mary:

> Initially our goal was to provide 50 percent of our training through online certification; we are currently running 75 percent online compliance. For some of our courses we went from 25 face-to-face sessions to on-line courses capped by a single live session, and we got the same number of people trained. This has allowed us to repurpose our training energy from dragging flip charts stands around the country to developing training.

· · · · · · · · · ·

6.4 Harnessing End Users to Add Value

End users hold an enormous wealth of information. The flow of information and informal learning within an organization can be enhanced by harnessing this informal knowledge base. As explained in Chapter 4.0, the main means of harnessing informal knowledge in a Web 2.0 world is by means of forums, blogs, and wikis. Although these means will never replace formal training, they might be a good tool to augment your learners' experience. Training managers need to understand what these technologies provide and determine whether and when they can be useful.

Some e-learning environments support the ability to easily add or access forums, blogs, and wikis. Many universities, for example, are providing virtual classrooms. They are recording lectures and making them available as podcasts. They are posting professors'

PowerPoint presentations, homework, and class assignments on the Web, and professors are using blogs as a way of annotating and commenting on subjects pertinent to those they are teaching and topics they are researching.

Although this Web environment facilitates accessing course material, it does not harness the end user. End users are harnessed when they can comment on the class and add additional thoughts to on-line forums. Many times learner comments can be beneficial to all the students in a course. How many times in a class does a class member illustrate the instructor's point with an example from personal experience or just ask an insightful question? By making it easy for students to make and to read comments by in a forum, informal learning can be harnessed and shared. This sharing of information adds value to an e-learning course by enriching the users' experiences.

Organizational structure highly affects the deployment and use of these types of tools, and training can be viewed and structured differently from one organization to another. Some organizations look at training as one aspect of the organization's content creation arm; one person, for instance, might manage training, documentation, and marketing communications writing. With this type of structure, managers typically look for ways to share and reuse the content that their people are creating. Documentation, marketing materials, and training can all originate from the same source documents. That is, if the organization uses a wiki to create its on-line product documentation, the training arm can link to the wiki as a source document within a training course. A wiki is a living document whose information customers and employees can annotate, add to, comment, or highlight, and this up-to-date information can also be used to keep training current.

6.5 Microcontent

A definite Web 2.0 trend is microcontent, that is, small training sessions that are taken as the need arises. The goal of microcontent is to move learners from training to learning, on the assumption that training is formal whereas learning goes on all the time. Informal training includes traditional sources like books, magazines, mentoring conversations, and trial and error. In the Web 2.0 workplace, these informal sources also include Web searches, Web sites, wikis, blogs, and forums.

As important as informal learning is, there is a benefit to the learner's having access to instructionally designed information. Without such structure and with so much information available, discerning which information is important and which is trivial can be difficult, not to mention which is current and which has expired or, most importantly what information is accurate and which is incorrect. Having pertinent information available, when needed, in a format conducive to learning is beneficial for most people. Generally these training sessions are not part of an employee's training curriculum. They may contain all the same elements found in longer courses. They may include tests that are included with the course to support learning but that are not used to track an employee's status. For instance, to access a corporate service, employees type the name of the service into the corporate search engine. A link to the service, along with a link to a short course on how to use the service, comes up at the top of the search. The employees take the short training and then use the service correctly.

6.6 Providing e-Learning Services Beyond the PC

If the goal of e-learning is to provide training to learners when they are ready and on the devices they have access to, it is very important to create content that works on all devices, on all browsers, and in all environments, making it accessible to the widest possible group of learners. That doesn't mean that all kinds of e-learning can be delivered to all kinds of devices. Specifically, Web course creators must recognize the capabilities and limitations of a currently very popular device: the smartphone.

When to Use Smartphones for e-Learning

As learning and training becomes more informal and moves toward microcontent, learners will be accessing the courses wherever they are. Typically this is in a mobile environment, that is, over a smartphone (a cell phone with a Web browser). For now, in today's environment, an organization has only two reasons for looking at creating training over phones:

1. To access learners where they are.
2. To provide training using the device the learner is using.

Training changes when the device shrinks. Before you decide to create training for smartphones, look at your learners' environments. To understand their environments, answer each of the following questions.

- Does your target market use cell phones?
- Do they currently text message?
- What do they currently read on their cell phone—nothing, short e-mails, long messages?
- Do they currently use cell phones to send e-mail?
- Do their cell phones have browsers (are they smartphones)?
- Does your organization pay for text messaging and browser access? (Be aware that cell phone providers charge for access and charge extra for smartphones.)
- Will your organization underwrite the expense when learners take courses using their smartphones?

The answers to these questions help you to identify whether your users can access mobile courses. If you receive mostly no answers to the questions, your audience does not have the technology in place to access mobile training. I recommend that on a yearly basis you ask your learners the same questions about their mobile use. Mobile technology and use are changing quickly. One year your mobile audience might only have phone calling capabilities, while a year later your mobile audience might have new phones with complete browser support.

Smartphone Limitations

Smartphones are more limited then PCs. Before creating training for a smartphone, course creators must clearly understand these limitations.

- The most important issue is the student experience. Cell phones provide a very distracted environment. Learners may be on a bus, in a train, at the store, eating lunch, or in a customer's waiting room.

- An audio plug-in may or may not work on learners' phones. If the course depends on audio, it's once again important to make sure that learners stay focused. If they are in an environment where people interrupt them, they may not stop and restart their audio player when interrupted; this means they have lost all the information presented while they are not paying attention. If the core of the course content is audio. it might be advisable to just make the course a podcast and not even bother with a visual component.

- The content should be suited to delivery on a cell phone. Most people do not want to read more than a few sentences per screen; content that is small, quick, and fast works best, such as memory joggers or sales lists, technical specifications, repeat subjects like corporate policies, and quick tests that are given in the field to ensure that employees remember important facts. For example, Telefonica created a series of Web pages for salespeople that were meant to be accessed from smartphones. Telefonica's field salespeople were responsible for a large, technical product line. The training organization created a features and benefits page on each product, along with top questions to ask customers. Salespeople in the field could easily access this information as a quick refresher before or during sales calls.

- The cell phone screen is very small, limiting what learners can see, and possibly making it difficult for them to read content and to take training over a cell phone. Adding audio does not solve the small screen problem, as we've seen.

Smartphone Screen Limitations

Cell screen size is a key factor in creating successful e-learning for a smartphone. When creating courses for delivery on smartphones, designers should keep a few guidelines in mind:

- Provide only a small amount of content on each page. Learners can horizontally scroll on a smartphone, but they may find it hard to follow lengthy text if they have to do too much scrolling. As a rule of thumb, never put more content on a page than what can be viewed on twice the screen size. So if an average screen supports 200 characters, the guideline is to use no more than 400 characters on a page.

- Choose visuals carefully. In addition to being small, the varying screen sizes of smartphones have different capabilities. Some browsers resize the fonts; other won't. Some browsers support zooming (the ability to resize the page in real time); other don't. Due to these limitations, be careful with visuals in general.

- When creating graphics, follow a couple of simple rules: Text should not be embedded in pictures because the screen is too small to permit it to be read. Keep the graphic small. If it is too big, the learner has to scroll horizontally and vertically to see it; this is frustrating because vertical scrolling is not supported on smartphones.

- Multimedia has limited smartphone support. Plug-ins like Flash, PDF, and any types of movies don't work on most smartphones.

Formatting for the Smartphone

If the same course is going to be used for PC and smartphone learners, create a separate style sheet or look and feel for each. There are many considerations when creating a site's look and feel (or branding) for smartphone delivery.

- Branding over a smartphone is very bare-bones because style sheet support is not standard or current.
- Avoid background graphics. The end users' ambient light is based very much on whether they are indoors or outdoors. Background graphics may make it impossible for them to read the screen in some light.
- Navigation elements need to be minimized. Graphic navigation icons like arrows might need to be changed to simple arrows or a descriptive word like "Next" or "Previous."
- Absolute positioning does not work on smartphones. Use good Web technology, and the course should work. Specifically, follow W3C recommendations like HTML and relative positioning (e.g., page resizing based on the browser size).
- Frames do work on smartphones. Some browsers handle frames by displaying additional frames below the main content.

Testing on the Smartphone

Tests work well on smartphones. However, creators have to work within the limitations of the device:

- The types of questions that work best are multiple-choice (multiple-selection) and true-or-false questions.
- Keep the question and answer choices short. Having too many questions on a test is unwieldy because they can easily become overwhelming on a small screen.
- Avoid questions that need manipulation like drag-and-drop.

- Limit the number of expected responses from students, some of whom might have limited keyboards. A limited keyboard might be fine for multiple-choice or true-or-false questions but not for text entry questions.

- If tests are being created and serviced, then most likely scores will be saved. When saving test questions, AICC [Aviation Industry CBT (Computer-Based Training) Committee] and SCORM (Sharable Content Object Reference Model)—standards designed to get courses talking with an LMS—need to work. They do work on iPhone, Minimo, and Symbion. They don't work on BlackBerry or MS Mobile, unless the LMS vendor has created a custom player for those environments. If so, each learner is required to download the player onto the cell phone. Having end users download a plug-in may become too big a barrier to getting the application adopted. ReadyGo SST does not require a player and works fine over all smartphone environments.

Smartphone Connections and Operating Systems

Many smartphones have access only to low-bandwidth services; that is, they may only have a 19.2-kilobyte-per-second (kbps) access, also referred to as dial-up access (what most people had on their computers back in the mid-1990s). Some smartphone users may get 56-kbps accesses, and still others can access WiFi broadband. Since access speeds are all over the place, make sure that course applications don't require high bandwidth and that there is no streaming content.

Currently, according to a 2007 study done by the Gartner Group, Symbian has 70 percent of the mobile operating system (OS) market; Linux has 15 percent, RIM's BlackBerry has 5 percent, and Microsoft has 5 percent. Smartphones are currently being used by about 10 percent of the U.S. population, and smartphone use is expected to rise to 50 percent by 2015.

Some smartphone operating systems and browsers work better then others, but all support the display of HTML and graphics.

Figure 6.1 Same page displayed on five different browsers.

(See Figure 6.1.) Course creators need to make sure the authoring tool they are using supports your learners' environment. Here is a survey of the different phones and their capabilities:

- BlackBerry is the most popular phone for business use. It supports zooming. However, the implementation of JavaScript is poor, it does not support flash, it ignores style sheets, and it provides no special handling of frames.

- The Minimo browser, developed by Mozilla (developers of the Firefox browser), is available for any Windows Mobile 5 and later device. Minimo is easy to install, provides full

JavaScript support, has decent zooming, and offers good style sheet support.

- The Symbian operating system and browser are from Nokia. It has really good zooming and a good browser.

- Microsoft Windows Mobile has lots of different versions, including CE5, Windows Mobile 5, and Windows Mobile 6. Its browser is poor, part of the really old IE 4/IE 5 browser. JavaScript works poorly. It does not support flash or zooming, it ignores style sheets, and it provides no special handling of frames.

- Apple's iPhone uses the Safari browser. It has great zooming and almost mouse-like support with its finger drag capabilities. Apple supports only Apple plug-ins; there is no support for Flash or Java.

- Palm has renamed its operating system Garnet. It has its own browser that does not respect style sheets very well. It does a nice job with frames, but it has weak support for dynamic HTML.

Authoring for Smartphone e-Learning

If forging ahead with creating courses for smartphones still sounds like a good idea, the first step is to find an authoring tool that works well with all the different devices. With a good authoring tool, your focus can be on creating content, not worrying whether works on the different devices. One tool that works well in every smartphone environment is ReadyGo WCB.

The next step is to obtain an emulator of each cell phone, which you can download from each vendor's Web site. With a working picture (emulator) of the cell phone on your PC, you can test your course in the learner's environment without having to purchase a cell phone. Using an emulator is as simple as using the real device, but downloading and installing an emulator are not always easy. A savvy computer person (likely from your organization's IT department) is needed to set them up.

• • • • • • • • • • •

Case Study: Granville Stephens

Granville Stephens is a publishing company, and one of their product lines consists of training courses for non-English speakers to learn English. Initially they created a series of books called "Learning English." They have augmented these books by producing courses that are available on podcasts and smartphones.

Granville Stephens's English education courses have been well received in Asia. Young Asians are very interested in learning English and represent a large segment of Granville Stephens' market. As they expand their Asian presence, Granville Stephens' goal is to provide training in the format that the learners are using. Smartphones have a very high market penetration in Asia, where many young people use smartphones.

As Granville Stephens expands its market reach, its goal is to provide its products in the format that its customers are using. They found that podcasts limited learning; only 10 percent of people are auditory learners, and the remaining 90 percent of the population have a 10 percent oral retention rate. Granville Stephens knew they could increase knowledge retention by creating language learning that includes visuals. What they came up with was an audio slide show format. The course displays the word, then a picture visually describing the word, with a voice-over of that word. The issue was converting the audio slide show to a format that would work on smartphones. Initially having created the slide show in PowerPoint, they transferred this to (tool name), then to (tool name), and saved it in (what format). This was a cumbersome process.

Additionally they wanted to produce a series of on-line tests for their learners. They wanted the learners to access the tests on the device they were using, most commonly a smartphone. The issue was how they would create smartphone-accessible courses that could be graded and tracked.

David Isaacson at Granville Stephens searched the Web for a better solution and found ReadyGo WCB and ReadyGo SST.

- *ReadyGo WCB* has five ways to pull PowerPoint material into a course. Because the tool is based on standard Web technologies, courses can be accessed by smartphones. To create a smartphone-accessible course, the creator has only to understand the limitations of viewing content on a small screen and to choose a smartphone template. Among the twenty-five ReadyGo templates is a smartphone template, which minimizes graphics and design features. The template has also been tested to work on the following PDAs and cell phones: Windows Mobile, Windows CE, BlackBerry, iPhone, Palm, and Symbian.
- *ReadyGo SST* lets you register students and saves student test scores, and it works with smartphones.

"ReadyGo's solution has made it easy for us to move to mobile devices. All we need to do is to create our courses and tests in ReadyGo WCB; everything works," states David.

· · · · · · · · · · · ·

6.7 The "Intel Inside" Approach

The "Intel Inside" phenomenon is the story of branding of the behind the scenes technology (Chapter 4.0). In e-learning, the behind-the-scenes technology is the authoring tool, graphic or simulation tool, and the LMS. Each of these vendors has an inherent interest in getting its name out to a wider audience. The Web 2.0 "Intel Inside" strategy is the kind used by vendors that are developing applications used in a hosted environment—an enabling technology—to brand the technology with their name on it. Specifically, the vendor wants the course, the learning object, or the system that delivers the course—the host—to have the brand name on it.

Look at the issue from the viewpoint of the application service provider. As such, you have to decide whether having the vendor's name on your service helps you meet your needs. When you create a word document, is "MS Word" branded on the document? When you create a presentation, is "MS PowerPoint" branded on it? Typically, organizations do not want the enabling technologies' branding on their documents; they want to their companies' name to be the branding force.

That said, it might still be worthwhile for you to deliver a learning solution with a vendor's name on it along with your name. A vendor that is trendy or that has a reputation for quality might give your solution more impact. Using a popular vendor might make learners more likely to use your solution. For example, learners might come to your training site and be willing to use your solution if it looks, feels, and works like a solution they already know.

6.8 New Technologies

The advent of a technology does not mean that the old is bad and the new is good. The ultimate goal is to get the end user to learn, not to demonstrate handiness with new technologies. A new technology is more effective only if it provides a better service than the previous one.

For example, at the time of writing, everyone is talking about podcasts, whose benefit is the ease of delivery: They are cheap to produce and easy to access. The issue is the quality of the content. A boring product training session is just as boring on a podcast as it was on a Walkman. To work well for organizations, podcasts should be professionally produced by audio specialists, narrated by professional voice-over actors, and entertaining. That's why the most popular podcasts are radio shows and music. Understanding learning styles before providing training via podcasts is also important. Only 10 percent of people are oral learners. By using a podcast and relying on only an oral form of training, you have marginalized 90 percent of your audience.

Another new technology is XML (Chapter 5.0). Again, at the time of writing, a lot of vendors are touting XML for training, even though there is no XML standard for training; that is, there is no standard set of values created for LMSs to store learner's information. If there were, then training databases created in one LMS could be interchangeably used by any other LMS. Many vendors who tout their XML capabilities are doing this just to make their proprietary systems sound open and flexible.

E-learning thinkers talk about content reusability, or being able to reuse elements developed in one course to create another. The theory behind this is intriguing, and the reality probably belongs in future conversations about artificial intelligence. The reason is that making all elements in a training courses reusable is not a trivial task. It requires a big, expensive database. And, it means that the course has to be reassembled, which does not negate the need to review the material to ensure that the course is smooth and instructionally sound. Most elements found in a course, saved independently, do not stand on their own. A proprietary form of XML can be used to identify course components, but you still need the database, and you still have to design, organize, and ensure the flow of a course. (More is said about breaking courses up into r-usable units in Chapter 9.0.)

6.9 What a 2.0 Course Looks Like

Web 2.0 courses is *not* a hodgepodge assembly of old methodologies delivered through new technologies, not just self-propelled PowerPoint presentations or CBT training presented on a PDA.

Web 2.0 courses should be true 2.0 courses, which:

- Provide just-in-time training.
- Are used as a resource—not as a one-time event.
- Last 15 to 20 minutes.
- Run smoothly on any configuration of device (high-resolution, portable) or PDA.
- Come through smoothly on all versions of Web browsers.
- Incorporate the best-of-breed techniques from Web design and instructional design.

The next few chapters provide tips and techniques for creating Web 2.0 courses.

6.10 Checklist

___ Questions to ask if you are considering the move to smartphone/cell phone training.

___ Does your target market use cell phones?

___ Do they currently text message?

___ What do they currently read on their cell phone—nothing, short e-mails, long messages?

___ Do they currently use cell phones to send e-mail?

___ Do their cell phones have browsers (i.e., are they smartphones)?

___ Does your organization pay for text messaging and browser access? (Be aware that cell phone providers charge for access and charge extra for smartphones.)

___ Will your organization underwrite the expense when learners take courses using their smartphones?

7.0

Components of an Effective Course

When managers are given a choice between having a course produced that meets goals and works well and putting great looking material online, many often choose having it look great. This choice might seem counterintuitive, but probably happens because most managers don't know how to identify a course that works well. Chapters 7.0 and 8.0 present features that work well in either traditional or rapid e-learning courses, but are particularly useful to the SME or trainer tasked with creating rapid courses.

Remember that traditional and rapid e-learning courses are different. Traditional e-learning has a large budget, which allows creators to buy the services of graphic artists and writers with the skills to turn standard corporate information into engaging, funny, ironic, or visually interesting material. Organizations need to pick and choose which courses are candidates for traditional e-learning.

The rest of the courses are left to the creative powers of an SME or trainer. Their rapid e-learning courses do not have to be boring, draining, or a waste of time. The basic principles in Chapters 7 and 8, when applied to e-learning courses, can make the material flow smoothly and maintain a learner's interest—even without a lot of experience with graphic design, writing resources, or the Web.

In addition, an author guideline document can be found as the appendix to this book. This document provides an author with a quick list of the guidelines to use when creating a course. These guidelines are discussed in detail in this chapter.

By the end of this chapter, you should be able to:

- Determining the right length of a course.
- Organize and lay out a course.
- Create core content pages.
- Explain the elements used to reinforce learning.
- Understand the importance of testing learners.
- Plan for certification testing.
- Write test questions.

7.1 Length of a Course

Taking courses on-line is very different from taking classroom training or reading a book. When creating a course, keep the learners' surroundings in mind. Most learners take courses in a very distracted environment. Typically they are sitting at their desk on their computer. Phones, people, e-mail, and in-baskets can all easily interrupt them. Most learners fit training in with their daily tasks, and course creators need to take this learning condition—and learners' limited time—into account and create courses that make it easy for learners to stay focused. E-learning courses should work well in an environment that is interrupt driven.

Understanding learners' attention spans and creating courses that play to learners' strengths also helps generate better results. Most people have difficulty concentrating for more than 15 to 20 minutes at a time. Providing chapters that are too long or courses with too many chapters overwhelms learners. Chunking material minimizes this effect. Here are some time-related guidelines:

- The rule of thumb for how long it takes a learner to complete material is 1 minute per page.
- A course or chapter of 15 to 20 pages should take about 15 to 20 minutes to complete.
- To create a course that works well in a busy person's schedule, start by breaking the course up into 15- to 20-minute segments. Do this either by creating a short 15- to 20-minute course or by breaking a longer course into 15- to 20-page, digestible chapters.
- Breaking a course into five chapters, each 15 to 20 pages in length, allows the learner to take one chapter a day and finish the course in one week. Learners have a sense of accomplishment when they can complete a chapter a day and a course a week.
- Break longer courses into separate modules, Each consisting of 5-, 15-, or 20-page chapters.

7.2 Layout and Course Organization

An old training adage that works well in e-learning is, "Tell them what you are going to tell them, tell them, and tell them what you told them." Following this advice, the basic layout and organization of a course should be easy for learners to navigate, and they should reinforce the information presented. A simple to follow and effective method for designing a course that reinforces learning is to break the material into the four-level structure explained in Chapter 2.0 (see Figure 2.4, page 48):

- Level 1: Course
- Level 2: Chapter
- Level 3: Page
- Level 4: Subpage

Level 1: Course

The front page (see Figure 7.1) should present the course name and a course summary ("Tell them what you are going to tell them . . ."). The summary can be either the learning objectives for the course or a high-level overview consisting of one to four sentences. The summary is important because:

- Asynchronous learning does not have an instructor in front of the classroom to confirm that the people are taking the right class, and many learners take a course without really knowing what is going to be presented.
- Learners learn information better when they have a frame of reference, which can consist of a simple set of goals or a summary of the material to be covered.

Level 2: Chapters

The same holds true for the first page in a chapter (see Figure 7.2). It really helps learners to have a frame of reference for the topics

Figure 7.1 Front page.

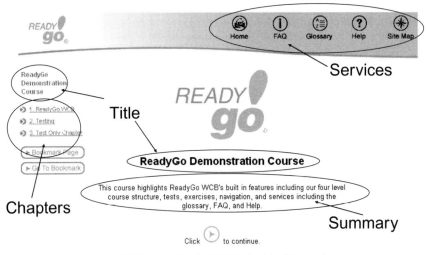

Figure 7.2 Chapter page.

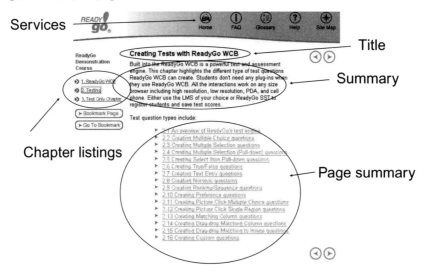

covered in each chapter. Frame each chapter with a chapter title and a summary or list of learning objectives. Also, optionally, provide a listing of the pages in that chapter—for a couple of good reasons:

- Books are broken into chapters and subsections to help readers understand what will be covered. The same rationale applies to e-learning. Designers and trainers can work together to bring clarity to a course by listing the subsections or pages in a chapter.

- In the future, having completed the course, learners can also use the chapter listing as a guide to access information directly.

Other course-wide organizational features that support the student and provide course structure are a services bar and a chapter listing.

- A *services bar* is an area that is always displayed and provides services available to the student while taking a course. Typically it contains the buttons for Help, FAQ, Glossary, Course map, and access to a wiki or blog.

- *Chapter listings* provide a hyperlink to other chapters in the course. Learners like to know how many chapters are in the course and have an idea of how long each chapter is. Just as when they are counting chapters in a book or the PowerPoint slides in a classroom course (how far along are we? how far do we have to go?), on-line learners have the same need for orientation. Learners feel empowered by visual clues that tell them how long the course is and where they are in it.

Level 3: Pages

The content resides at the third layer in our structure, the page ("Tell them . . ."). All content, or course, pages should have a chapter and page number (see Figure 7.3, before the page title). For the same reason that books and handouts have numbering and paging systems (parts, chapters, text sections), we should number on-line courses. Learners like knowing where they are. Numbering also

Figure 7.3 Content page.

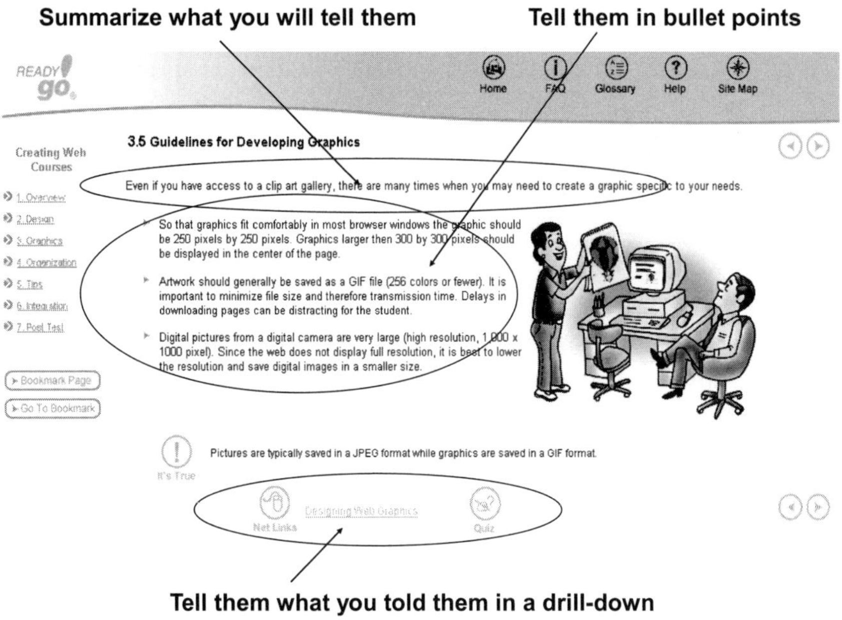

Summarize what you will tell them   **Tell them in bullet points**

Tell them what you told them in a drill-down

makes it easier for learners to reference a page when they want to discuss a concept or ask a question.

The content page should provide:

- A *summary:* This frames the material and provides an easy way for course creators to start a new topic.

- *The core material as bulleted points:* People read material on paper differently then they read on-line. On-line learners scan for important points. The small phrases used in Power Point slides don't work well because you do not have an instructor bringing the outline to life. What works best is writing like a journalist: Highlight conclusions, and then follow with more detail.

- *Optional information at the fourth level, drill-down elements:* Detailed content should be provided only if the learner wants it, by providing optional information in drill-down pages.

The bulleted points feature is particularly important in e-learning, Providing information in paragraph form is overwhelming for learners and does not enhance retention. Breaking the content into bulleted points helps to increase knowledge retention. An interesting study was done about 10 years ago by Jakob Nielsen, PhD, a distinguished Sun Microsystems engineer and a pioneer in the field of usability (http://www.useit.com/alertbox/9710a.html). In this study he takes a technically written paragraph and increases on-line reading retention by simplifying the content. He increases the learner's retentions by 48 percent when he converts an unreadable paragraph into bulleted points. He then stripped out the statistics found in the original paragraph, broke the material into bulleted points, and increased the learner's subject retention by 124 percent.

Another good reason for using bulleted points has to do with the nature of the Web itself. Although a Web page is not limited like a page of paper or a PowerPoint screen and a Web page can be scrolled if it does not fit all on the screen at once, a very long Web page still does not work well. In fact, it is cumbersome for users. Therefore, it is helpful to break material into chunks. Here are some tips:

- With a 1024×768 display screen and type in 10- or 12-point fonts, about 400 words, or 30 lines of text, can be easily displayed.

- Never make a page longer then two screen lengths. If a page is too long, it becomes unwieldy for the learners, who tend to loose their place and become overwhelmed. Also learners may want to read a section that relates to a previous point or reread the previous point. Navigating to an earlier page is much easier than trying to scroll through a very long page.

- Avoid using multiple columns. Many times people just forget to read the second column. Having scrolled down to read the first column, learners don't always remember to scroll back to the top of the page to read the next column. One long paragraph that requires scrolling down works better then two or more narrow columns that require scrolling down and up and down again.

Level 4: Subpages

Level 4 pages, or drill-down page, can be used to reinforce learning ("Tell them what you told them . . ."). These pages supplement the bulleted items on the content pages. Often, a course creator can use the source material used to create a classroom course as the information for the drill-down pages in e-learning.

Drill-down pages may be:

- An article
- A link to a Web resource
- An exercise
- A simulation
- A movie
- A test

Drill-down pages should be optionally accessed for simple reason. Many times learners bring different levels of experience and training to the same course. It is frustrating for some students to take a course made up of a series of daisy-chained flash simulations presenting a lot of things they already know. They must wait for each simulation series to be completed so that they can continue with the course. Experienced learners want to go quickly through the course, stopping when they reach a new idea or to take a test. Expert learners may want to see the supporting information used to make the assumptions presented on a page within a course. At the same time, new learners may need to go through each page in detail and need supporting information to reinforce a topic. Drill-down pages can therefore accommodate a range of learners by making the additional information optional as detail for the new learner or as backup information for the more inquisitive learner.

Here's an example. At every hospital in the United States, every year, everyone who works at the hospital needs to be JCAHO certified, that is, the hospital needs to provide training on their processes and procedures. This training includes topics like disaster recover and hand washing, and every hospital has different procedures. In all cases, however, the training has to accommodate a range of experience levels:

- Nurses who have worked at the hospital for many years are experienced in the benefit of careful hand washing and should know that it is necessary. They can get through the mandatory hand washing course quickly.

- Employees who are new to health care and who have never worked in an environment that requires hand washing need more time to go through the course. New learners benefit from choosing to view a video showing someone washing the hands properly.

- If the hospital has just begun to allow hand sanitizers in some wards, even experienced employees may want to read this section in more detail.

- An epidemiologist may want to read the source document from the Centers for Disease Control that provides statistics defining why hand sanitizers are safe in certain circumstances.

7.2 Presentation Options for Content Pages

Course designers have a number of presentation options. By providing information in multiple, optional formats, course creators make it easier for learners of different skill levels to use the same course and to get what they need from it. They also turn the course into a useful, ongoing resource. After taking the course, when the learners are back on the job, they may be asked to perform a procedure they learned. They may not remember the details of that procedure, but they do remember that the course shows how to perform the it. All they have to do is access the course as a resource.

Tours

For courses that are teaching multistep skills like hand washing or using the organization's new computer system, providing information in multiple formats is helpful. If the course's goal is to teach new employees how to use the company computers, the course creator can develop a screen-snapshot simulation, also referred to as a tour. (See Figure 7.4.) A tour is a little movie that shows the mouse moving on a screen performing the on-line procedure that the learner will use.

Step-by-Step

Often, people who view tours of procedures that they will need to use stop the tour so that they can write down each of the steps. To make it easy on the learner, the course creator convert the tour and to a step-by-step. Each step in the tour should be accompanied by a table with a description of what is being performed and a picture of what that screen looks like. Learners can then print

Figure 7.4 Tour and step-by-step.

Flash Tour

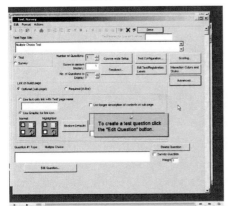

Step-by-Step

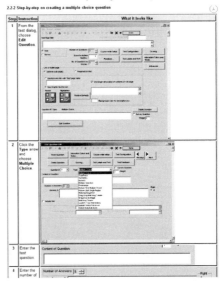

the page and use it when they are actually on the screen performing the procedure.

Self-Assessment

A self-assessment can be used to get learners to think about a subject or to understand their reaction to a situation. We commonly see self-assessments in magazines. For example, a health magazine may include a self-assessment to help readers ascertain their physical age. The self-assessment may ask how many days a week you exercise, at what rate you exercise, and for how long. It may also ask you to enter in your BMI (body mass index) and whether you suffer from high blood pressure or diabetes. On the basis of this information, you are given a score. A score of 0–5 may mean that you are 20 years older then your chronological age; a score of 20–25 may indicate that you are off-the-charts healthy and will live to 105. This same type of self-assessment can be used in e-learning.

Simulations

Simulations run from simple to complex and from cheap to very expensive, and so the training budget has a lot to do with they type of simulation that you can afford. Given that a professionally produced and sophisticated simulation can easily cost $50,000, high-end simulations are usually found in traditional e-learning courses.

With such a large expenditure at stake, course creators, in the early stages of design, should identify what types of simulations are needed to illustration the concepts being presented and to support the course in achieving its learning objective. Then they need to research whether their budget supports the required level of simulation. If they don't have the budget to create what they want, they need to figure out how else can they present the concept. If there is no other way to present the concept, they should consider making this section of the course a hands-on workshop.

One of the biggest mistakes course creators make is to try to make their courses more interesting just by adding simulations or games that do not directly support the learning objective. Many organizations include games in their courses just to make them more interesting. Course designers, however, really have to think through the viability of this tactic. In a business environment, games annoy many adults, not entertain them. In particular, just to make a course more interesting, course creators sometimes add word games to courses that have nothing to do with language skills. Except in an English course, stay away from games like crossword puzzles, hangman, or Scrabble. One reason is these games do not built the intended skills.

Another reason is that they can even alienate some learners. Most learners did not major in English, and, for some employees, English may be a second language. Because word games test English skills, not the concepts presented in the course, they can frustrate and turn off most learners. One company created a series of courses for their retail workers that included lots of games. Although the courses were well received, employees spent hours playing the on-line games. Unfortunately, no productivity increases are associated with all this game playing. The employees just liked playing games instead of working.

That does not mean games cannot work in e-learning. It just means that you need to think through the skills you are attempting to teach and come up with a game that reinforces them. If you can't find a relevant game to match the skill, then forget about games and just teach the skill.

7.3 Why Test Learners?

Testing is a very important course attribute for most organizations. Trainers and human resources managers tend to focus a lot of energy on testing. When asked why they want to test learners, they respond:

- "How can I rank and measure employees?"
- "How can I be assured that they have taken the course?"
- "How can I be assured that they know the material that was covered?"

So here is a test question for you: Are tests used in e-learning to:

1. Identify knowledge?
2. Frame information?
3. Identify comprehension?
4. Get the learners thinking?
5. Help learners retain new information?
6. All of the above?

Testing is, simply, an easy and excellent way to engage the learner. Figure 7.5 shows a continuum for course content that ranges from very passive to very active.

Figure 7.5 Spectrum of passive to active content.

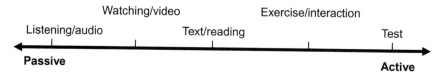

- The most passive way to provide information is to read to learners. Reading to adults at best engages their ears.

- To make courses a little more active, you can show learners a movie. Now they need to maintain visual and auditory awareness.

- A more active way to engage the learner is to have them read the material, because it forces them to actually pay attention, not just passively listen.

- Exercises can be even more active. If they are done right, they engage learners. (Note: Most exercises created by SMEs or trainers seem to be more passive than the active, graphic, professionally designed exercises created in traditional e-learning courses.)

- The most consistently active way to engage learners in rapid e-learning is to ask them a question. Not only do they need to pay attention, but they are also forced to process information and respond.

What this means is that test questions can be used any time during a course, and they are particularly effective when employees early on to frame the information. When presenting a new concept, the course might ask a learner a couple of up-front test questions on the subject. Often, learners are familiar with the subject or think they know the content to be presented. For example, this section started with a test question. Did you take the test? What did you answer? The correct answer is that all the options are correct. Did you get the right answer before reading on?

Engaging learners is easiest when you ask questions that make learners think and that tests their knowledge about a subject. Another benefit is that they get hooked when they get the question wrong.

A test question works better on-line because learners see only what is on the screen and need to click a button to read ahead. On-line, a test question is an easy way to frame the conversation and engage learners. Although tests and questions can be used for measuring, in e-learning they can also be used for a whole lot more. Effective trainers don't just tell; they engage and ask. Even when removed from a typical classroom, learners need to be engaged.

7.4 Certification Testing

Many organizations produce certification training, that is, they need to certify that certain employees have been given required information and that they have demonstrated proficiency in the subject area.

The goal of any certification course is to have every employee score 100 percent, and there is a surefire way to accomplish this aim: Give a test question every couple of pages—but make question relevant. The question should identify the most important point and ask the student a straightforward question on this point. If learners get the in-chapter test question correct, they continue with the course; if they get it wrong, they are sent back to the content page.

In-chapter test questions help on many levels:

- They reinforce the information presented.
- They slow learners down so that they aren't just clicking through a course.
- They make learners think about what is being presented.
- They stimulate them not only receive but also to transmit what they have learned.
- They highlight what is really important.

Reinforcing material through a series of tests is a great organizational solution to use anytime the training goal is 100 percent on a final exam.

- At the end of each chapter, give the student all the in-chapter questions again, this time in a chapter test.
- At the end of the course, give the students all or a subset of the questions found in the course.

By the third time learners see the same question, they should know the answer. Testing them along the way ensures that they retain and understand the most important points of the course.

As an added bonus, certification testing helps to indemnify the organization. Suppose, for example, an employee scores 100 percent on a course about their company's drug and alcohol policy. Later the employee is in a drug-related accident on company property. The company can use the results from the test to prove that the employee was provided the corporate policy and demonstrated proficiency in understanding it, thereby helping to indemnifying the organization.

7.5 Tips for Writing Test Questions

Test-Taking Tactics

By the time we start working, many of us have taken countless tests. So, when creating e-learning tests, we should incorporate the test-taking tactics we were taught in school:

- Read all the test questions first.
- Answer the questions you know first.
- Go back to see whether you can answer the questions you did not answer in the first pass.
- When reading a multiple-choice question, scratch off the answers you know are wrong first.

Online tests should allow learners to use these test skills. Display test questions on a single page or grouped together on a series of single pages, so that learners can read a series of questions before making their choices. Avoid serving learners one test question at a time.

Test-Taking Tools

If the course's testing tool does not allow for more then one question on a page, if you cannot place tests anywhere in a chapter, or if it is does not support end-of-chapter and end-of-course tests, find a better tool. A good tool should also help you indicate which tests are to be used to reinforce information and which are to be used as part of the certification process.

Storing Answers

Storing learners' answers to test questions might be useful even if the test is not for certification. Storing answers to all test questions helps when:

- It comes time to review how often learners need to retake tests.
- Investigating an problem employee incident (like the drug-related accident in the preceding example).
- A course creator needs to see whether specific test questions are frequently marked incorrect—questions that might be confusing or need better explanations.

Types of Questions

A course creator can deploy many types of questions, always keeping mind that the goal of the test is to demonstrate learner proficiency. The best test questions are simple, straightforward, and focused on the material at hand. They may be boring, but multiple-choice and true-or-false questions are usually the most effective. Here are other things to keep in mind:

- When used appropriately, *graphics* can be very helpful in a test. The question should contain a visual if the visual was part of the presentation in the course or if you are testing on a visual concept. For example, if the skill required is how to identify two classifications of widgets, create a test question that shows multiple widgets and have the learner designate which fall into each classification.

- When creating test questions, ask *salient questions*; avoid obscure ones. Unless the test is about reading comprehension, testing on obscure references or trivia is not useful. The key is to test learners on the most important topics.

- The old *KIS (keep it simple)* model applies. Questions should be as simple as possible: no double negatives or words not commonly used in the daily work environment. The goal is to ascertain learners' knowledge, not their language skills.

- When providing answers—or feedback—give *extended explanations* of why one multiple-choice selection is better than the others. In addition, feedback should be relevant. It should not just give the correct answer but also explain why a specific option was incorrect or why the answer was correct.

- Also, *alternate answer choices* so that learners don't always choose answer B, for example.

- Limit the number of test questions on a test page to 10 or 15, never more than 20 questions. Scrolling through a very long test page is difficult, causing learners to miss a question. If an exam absolutely must have, say, 50 test questions, logically break the test into four or five separate test pages.

7.6 Checklist

__ Course length checklist:

1. Five chapters per course.
2. No more then 15 to 20 pages per chapter.
3. No more then 15 test questions on one page.

___ Four levels of a course and the elements found on each page type.

1. Course:
   - Title.
   - Summary/course objectives.

2. Chapter:
   - Title.
   - Summary/chapter objectives.

3. Page:
   - Title.
   - Subject summary.
   - Bullet points.
   - Access to subpage.

4. Subpage:
   - Title.
   - Information, movie, exercise, test question(s).

___ Is your test being used to:

1. Identify knowledge?
2. Frame information?
3. Identify comprehension?
4. Get the learners thinking?
5. Help learners retain new information?

Graphics and Multimedia

Most courses have graphics and multimedia, but do these features add to the course, detract from it, or just slow it down? This chapter gives you an idea of how to select the type of graphics and multimedia that is more than eye candy and that supports the course goals. The aim is to help you select the graphics that best work in e-learning courses. In addition, you'll learn about multimedia, including the limitations of multimedia and when and how to use it effectively.

 By the end of this chapter, you should be able to:

- Distinguish among the types of computer graphics.
- Select the graphic formats that work best on the Web.
- Understand the basics of copyright law.
- Use the guidelines for developing graphics.
- Choose the right kind of audio for Web courses.
- Explain multimedia uses.

8.1 Computer Graphics

Computer graphics are two- and three-dimensional images that are created, saved in a specific format, and viewed on a computer. Sometimes the software used to create the graphic dictates the format that the graphic has to be saved in, and other times the graphic artist can decide on the format. (Some graphic software programs support many different types of graphic files, that is, a file created in one format can be read and saved in a different one.)

There are many types of graphic formats, and each was developed for specific reasons. Graphic formats are created by software companies, and most formats started out as a way to save a file in the specific software package—such as the .ai format in Adobe Illustrator. The file format is identified by the two- to four-letter extension in the file name, such as .doc, .pdf, or .jpg. Some graphic formats, such as .reps or .ai, were developed to work with high-resolution printers. Other graphic formats can be displayed on a computer screen but cannot be viewed in a Web browser, such as .wpg or .tiff.

Every graphic format has its strengths and weaknesses. Some store images in very high resolution and work well with printers, whereas others are optimized to download fast so that they work well on computer screens. Web browsers support a small number of graphic formats.

Graphic formats are different from multimedia formats.

- Multimedia formats support movies and audio, and they require a plug-in.
- Graphic formats are for images and are natively supported by the browser; that is, they don't require a plug-in, and all browsers can display these graphics.

8.2 Web Graphic Formats

The three most common graphic formats that browsers can view are GIF (.gif), JPEG (.jpg), and PNG (.png). All three formats can be displayed by all browsers without downloading a plug-in. Generally, GIF and PNG files are used for graphics, and JPEGs are used for photographs.

GIF (Graphics Interchange Format)

GIF (Graphics Interchange Format) is probably the most popular graphic format on the Web. GIF is a patented file format that supports 256 (8-bit) colors and is generally used for a wide range of graphics. It has three major features that make it popular:

1. *Interlacing* is a method of storing the image so that, when it is displayed, its quality is improved by several passes: The first pass provides a shadow of the image, the second pass fills in the image, and the third pass completes the image. For large graphics, interlacing lets the learner get an idea of the associated image before it has all been constructed.

2. With *transparency*, the graphic designer can designate one color of the image as transparent, allowing the text or other images beneath the GIF to be visible. Or the background of the graphic can be designated as transparent, making the picture look as if it is floating on the page, that is, not in a frame.

3. The ability to simulate *animation*, which is actually a sequence of GIFs displayed at intervals so that they appear to be moving. Animated GIFs are used when you want a moving image but your learner's environment does not support plug-ins.

PNG (Portable Network Graphics)

PNG (Portable Network Graphics) is a patent-free replacement for GIF. It supports many colors, is generally used for a wide range of graphics, and can also be used to save photographs.

JPEG or JPG (Joint Photographic Experts Group)

JPEG or JPG (Joint Photographic Experts Group) is a patent-free file format that supports 16 million (24-bit) color. With its high resolution capabilities, JPEG is generally used for photographs.

8.3 Choosing File Formats for Web Graphics

Web Requirements

Historically, most graphics received from a marketing department or a graphic artist were meant for print. In the past you may have directly brought very large graphics into your PowerPoint presentations, where they work fine.

The Web is different. PowerPoint slides reside on a trainer's PC. They are not intended to be transmitted over the Internet, as are e-learning courses. On the Internet, file size makes a difference. No matter how big your network is, every administrator will tell you that if you make your Web pages small, the network will work faster, and your learner will have a better experience. A large graphic affects the learner's experience because it increases the time it takes for a Web page to download and display. Most learners have a short attention span, and they consider a page broken if it takes longer then eight seconds to display. Web learners don't want to wait 10 to 20 seconds for a large graphic to download. The goal is to have graphics that download in one to two seconds.

The greater number of colors in and the higher resolution of a graphic make it clearer, but they also make it larger, and the large file size means a slow download. Therefore, in creating graphics for the Web, there is a sweet spot between resolution and size when a fairly high-resolution graphic downloads quickly. Therefore, choose the appropriate graphic files format and to optimize graphics so that they download fast, but still look nice—as small as possible while maintaining the graphic's clarity.

Downsizing Images

Despite Web requirements, most graphics supplied by an artist or a marketing department are not in the .gif format. To optimize the files, you need a graphic program that easily optimizes graphics so that they can download fast without compromising quality. Corel Paint Shop Pro is very simple to use and has all the features you should ever need. To make the image work on the Web, you need to change the graphics format, and you can usually do that in a couple of ways:

- You can drastically reduce the size of the graphic just by bringing it into the graphic tool in the original format and saving it as a .gif.

- You can reduce the resolution (the dots per inch or dots per centimeter). When you change the image from, say, 120 dpi to 60 dpi, the file size drops to one-quarter its original size. In terms of download, if the larger graphic would have taken 20 seconds, the smaller version will take five.

- Another option is to choose fewer colors. This technique works well with illustrations, but not for photographs. Most graphic programs give you the choice of saving a file as a 16-color, 256-color, or 24-bit (16,777,216-color) image. The more colors the graphic contains, the larger it is. Most illustrations display well on the Web at 256-color, but most photographs need to be saved as 24-bit. When changing the number of colors, look at the graphic before and after the change to make sure it did not lose too much resolution. The difference is obvious when printing out the graphics, although there might not be any visual difference on the monitor.

- You can also enter the size of the graphic in the Width and Height attributes dialog box found on most graphic interfaces in authoring tools. Dropping the size of graphics speeds up their display because the browser knows how to lay out the page before downloading the file.

Digital Photographs

Course creators often run around the office with a digital camera and take pictures of people at work. These digital photographs work great in an e-learning course. Having pictures of coworkers personalizes the course and engages learners, who enjoy seeing coworkers in the courses they are taking.

Photographs are typically saved and stored on your digital camera as JPEGs—which can be huge. The photographs are very high resolution and meant for very high-resolution printers. When using photographs in an e-course, you have to shrink them so that they display fast and fit on the screen.

Optimizing a photograph is easy with a graphic tool. A typical digital photograph may be 1280 × 1860 pixels (a pixel is one point or dot in a graphic) and 300 dpi (dots per inch); a photograph that big might have a 1 megabyte of file size. When the size of the photograph is decreased to 400 × 600 and 70 dpi, the file might now be 70 kilobytes. The optimized picture is a third the size of the original allowing, it to be optimally viewed in the learner's window, and it downloads 14 times faster. Just be aware that a Web-optimized photograph displays well on a computer screen but looks funny if printed on a high resolution printer.

Stock Photographs

Taking photographs of coworkers might not be realistic or possible. In that case, a couple sites on the Web provide stock photographs. Among such sites are Istockphoto and Fotolia. Istockphoto has more diverse photographs, and Fotolia has more pictures of the same person with different expressions.

Instead of using bulleted points to express a concept, you can present the same information in comic book fashion, that is, by putting balloons over employee or stock photos and having the faces in the photos speak to each other to relay the information. (See Figure 8.1.) A $25 tool like ComicLife enables you to make talk balloons and pictures look right. Using stock photos or employee photographs to lighten up a course is a creative way to make your courses more interesting.

Unfortunately for course developers with a small budget, hiring

Figure 8.1 Stock photos.

artists and course developers to lighten up a course turns a rapid e-learning course into the price of its traditional big brother. However, a lot of elements used by professionals can be deployed by SMEs and trainers when they build rapid e-learning. Deploying these elements takes time and thought, but they make your courses more interesting.

8.4 Basics of Copyright Law

Most course creators get their course graphics from a variety of sources. They may copy and paste existing graphics from their PowerPoint presentations, access a clip art gallery, hire an artist, or use pictures of coworkers taken with a digital camera. Before using a graphic, however, your organization must have the legal rights to it. Here are some considerations when you are gathering graphics for your latest course:

- Purchasing a clip art gallery or accessing a Web site with stock photos requires agreement to their terms and conditions, and a fee may be required.

- Graphics you see on someone else's Web site or the graphics in Google Images are legally owned by someone else. You might be able to grab a graphic and save it to your desktop, but you may not necessarily legal use it on your Web site.

- Most employees sign a waiver when they are hired that states any materials they create belongs to their organization. Some organizations include the use of employee images in that waiver; that is, the organization can legally use an employee's image in any marketing pieces. Before you take pictures of coworkers to use in an e-learning course, check with human resources or the legal department to be sure that this waiver is in place. If not, you may have to create a waiver, which each employee has to sign before the image can be used in any course (on-line or traditional).

- When using an outside artist, you have to check the legal agreement to ensure that your organization has the right to use the artist's graphics on your Web site. This also includes all materials provided by the marketing department.

Take the extra time to make sure that all graphics are used legally. You don't want a course you produced cited in a copyright infringement case.

8.5 Guidelines for Employing Graphics

Once you decide to include graphics in an e-learning course, their sizes must be determined, regardless of whether they come from a clip art gallery, marketing, or a graphic artist. When importing graphics into a course, the goal is to create graphics that fit comfortably in the learner's browsers. Learners should not have to have scroll to view the graphic.

Many course creators embed a graphic in their text or create a page with two columns. On two-column pages, one column should consist of text or bulleted points, and the second column should have a graphic. If a page has text on one side and graphics on the other side, the graphics should be about 250×250 pixels. If the graphic is larger than 300×300 pixels, it should be displayed in the center of the page, where the text is above or below the graphic.

Laying out two column pages for paper documents is different from the layout for the Web. Graphic artists like to vary the placement of graphics so that the page looks interesting; they may place the graphic on the right of the text and then later on the left. On a Web page, it is difficult for people to read text if the graphic is on the left and the text is on the right. (See Figure 8.2.) Since we read from left to right, our eyes reach the graphic and then move down without moving past the graphic and reading the text on the other side. To get people to read the text, place it on the left and the graphic on the right.

Figure 8.2 Two-column page.

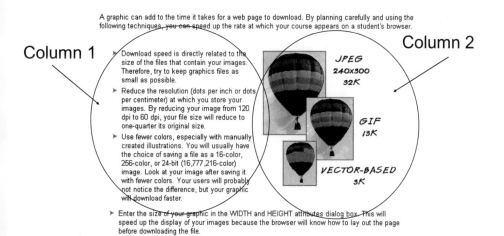

Here are some other guidelines:

- The optimal size for a graphic displayed in the center of the page, with text below or above it, is 400×400 pixels. (See Figure 8.3.)

Figure 8.3 Size of multimedia.

Logo   Picture with bullets

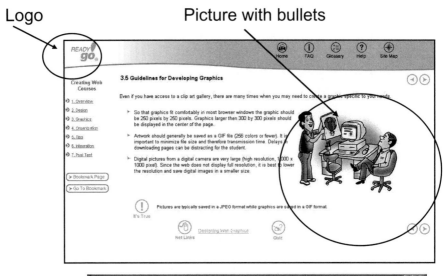

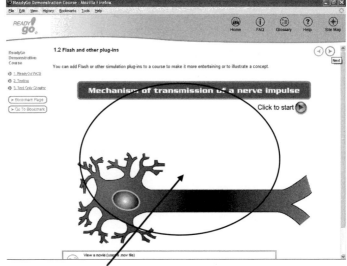

Picture, PDF, or Flash below or above bullets

- If full-page viewing is the goal because you are displaying a page in Adobe Acrobat (.pdf), the size should no larger then 800×600.

- Brand the course by placing your company logo in the upper left-hand corner of each page or at least on the first page of your Web course. This graphic should be about 50×50 pixels.

8.6 Audio for Web Courses

Audio is a multimedia element that should be used sparingly in courses. Many employees either do not have the equipment to hear audio at work because the IT department has disabled the audio, or they do not have headphones. Even if your organization supports audio and employees are given headphones, think twice about deploying audio for your courses (or at least do not make it an integral part of the course). There are several reasons:

- Audio gives learners a pass at paying attention to a course. When the audio comes on, learners move their eyes from the course to something else on their desk or desktop within four to eight seconds from the time the audio starts.

- Learners find it easier to miss audio segments than other segments of a course due to interruptions. If the learner is listening and someone comes into their workspace to ask a question, the learner might not stop the audio. The course is now second to the interruption, and typically the learner loses all the content discussed while they were interrupted.

- Having a narrator read what is on the screen is very annoying to adults. Having a narrator read words that are different from what is on the screen is more than annoying; it is very confusing.

- Depending on the study, somewhere between 10 and 25 percent of people learn from audio, whereas 30 to 65 percent of the population learn visually.

- The average college graduate reads at 250 to 300 words per minute, with 70 percent comprehension, and the average person can speaks 125 to 150 words per minutes.

- According to the Learning Pyramid, listeners retain only about 5 percent of what they hear in a lecture.

Despite all these shortcomings, course creators maintain that audio is easy for them to create. I dispute this claim. An SME, with the help of a training professional and using the guide in the appendix of this book, should be able to add the needed instructional design to a 90-page PowerPoint presentation in about four hours. Included in the four hours are all the elements needed for drill-downs and tests. The upgraded PowerPoint presentation can then be poured into a rapid e-learning tool (such as ReadyGo WCB), and the course creator can create graphics, identify clip art, or even create or higher someone to create simulations. The whole process takes fewer then eight hours, typically spread over a week.

Nevertheless, organizations simply add audio to their PowerPoint courses and add audio to them. They maintain that the process of creating, optimizing, and including audio in a PowerPoint presentation takes about 15 hours (five hours for SMEs to record themselves, plus eight hours to clean up and optimize the recording). At the end of this process is a PowerPoint presentation with an SME reading the material.

In additional to the course taking twice as long to produce, learners might take twice as long to take it, and learner retention might drop by 50 to 90 percent. Which type of course do you think a manager at your organization would choose?

- Course A: Takes 45 minutes to take, and the employee retains about 10 percent of the material.

- Course B: Takes 15 to 25 minutes to take, and the employee retains 50 to 75 percent of the material.

If you chose Course B, you chose a nonaudio course, instructionally designed for the Web.

So an audio course doesn't take less time to produce; it's just easier because course creators don't have to think about instructional design. They can depend on tools they already know, like PowerPoint.

Consider your commitment to e-learning if you are choosing poor solutions because they're the easiest for you—not the best for the learner. Having learners read material may not sound exciting, but it makes for a course that is less passive, that increases learning retention, and that take less time to complete. Audio works well when it is presented as an option and is used to explain complex graphics that are not explained in the associated text.

8.7 Multimedia Recommendations

Although theoretically many types of multimedia can be integrated into any Web course, realistically deploying multimedia has its limitations. Multimedia is generally defined as images that move, commonly videos and simulations.

Videos

You can send a video to a learner in two ways:

1. *Streaming video* is a technology similar to that of cable or satellite TV, except the video is sent over the Internet or your company's intranet.
2. An *embedded* (or *downloaded*) *video* is a video file that is sent to the browser with the Web page and then played.

Streaming video requires a video server, and it is deployed if you have lots of videos or many very long videos. If your organization already has a video server and the videos you want to play in a course are on it, the video can just be linked your e-learning course. If your organization doesn't have a video server, the video would have to be saved as a file (e.g., .mpg) and pulled into the course.

Videos are an excellent way to explain a specific task visually or to show how a specific task works, but keep them brief. Taking Web courses is not like watching TV and relaxing on your couch. By about four minutes into a video (or simulation or flash presentation), most people have stopped paying attention. Learners have a two- to four-minute attention span. That's probably why most videos on MTV and YouTube are about that length.

So break videos into short segments that last one to two minutes. If you have to show 10 minutes of video, chunk it into five two-minute segments. Learners will pay attention to five two-minute segments but zone out when watching a 10-minute segment.

Also, save your video files in flash (.swf) format. Flash is supported on most browsers and is allowed into most organizations through firewalls and networks, whereas most video formats, like .mpg, are not.

• • • • • • • • • • • •

Case Study: Highline Public Schools

A course in which video was used effectively was developed by Highline Public Schools, a public school district located just south of Seattle, Washington. Highline has nearly 18,000 students whose families speak over 80 different languages. The district developed a training course for monolingual English-speaking teachers and administrators to enable them to communicate more effectively with non-English-speaking families through a bilingual interpreter. You can see the course on-line at http://www.speakyourlanguages.com/training/. The training course on how to work with a foreign language interpreter was enthusiastically received. The course dramatically improved peoples' ability to work with interpreters and enabled them to overcome their fear of communicating with non-English speakers. The course is not highly produced, but it follows good instructional techniques, using short videos to highlight concepts. The use of video in the course makes the course more interesting and illustrates the points being presented.

• • • • • • • • • • •

Flying Bullets

Flying bullets are not multimedia, but some course creators think that the flying bullets make their courses more interesting. Flying bullets work well in an instructor-led session, including synchronous e-learning, but they work poorly in asynchronous e-learning. Just as audio can be frustrating to asynchronous learners, waiting for a bullet to fly onto the page before getting to the information can be frustrating too.

The goal is to provide students with quality, easy-to-use training material. Don't get caught up in the bling of multimedia. Use multimedia prudently to make the course more effective.

PowerPoint to Flash

Many companies are turning their PowerPoint courses into Flash and posting them on the Web. The rationale is that they already have a lot of PowerPoint presentations and are looking for a fast way to get the content onto their Web sites. However, PowerPoint does not stand on its own; it meets none of the design considerations discussed in this book. Most tellingly, employees, when faced with taking a voice-annotated PowerPoint-to-Flash presentation, have learned to turn it on, walk away, and come back when it is over—or just flip through the course as quickly as possible—before taking the final exam.

For employees who really want to learn the material, spend the time making it a quality experience.

- Don't read to them; provide them with a course that is engaging and enlightening.
- If you are trying to get just facts out to your learner population, put the material on a wiki.
- Decide which PowerPoint presentations have relevant information and need to be turned into e-learning courses; then spend the time to create an effective course.

- Archive the rest of the PowerPoint presentations natively so that they are available to employees on demand.

8.8 Checklist

___ Three types of graphic formats:

1. GIF.
2. JPEG (JPG).
3. PNG.

___ Copyright law:

1. Do you have a release for using an employee's picture in your course? Do all employees sign a waiver when they are hired that states their image can be used by the company?
2. Do you have a waiver with your graphic artist stating that you can use his or her work on the Web?
3. Do the clip or stock images in your course require a fee for use in a course?

___ Graphic size recommendations:

1. Logo in the upper left: 50×50 pixels.
2. Graphic in a two-column format: 250×250 pixels.
3. Graphic in a single column: 400×400.
4. PDF file: no larger than 600 pixel width by 800 pixel length.

Standards and Integration

Everyone in e-learning bandies about terms like "AICC," "SCORM," "SCOs," and "reusability." Do you understand the ramifications of the technologies and ideas behind these terms? This chapter gives you background and insight so that you don't just say terms but understand how they can be used to build better course infrastructure.

 By the end of this chapter, you should be able to:

- Understand what you need to know about standards and integration.
- Explain the basics of the major integration standard AICC.
- Describe the basics about the major integration standard SCORM.
- Explain SCOs.
- Describe the importance of shareable, reusable content.
- Understand how courses behave.
- Identify what questions to ask.
- Recognize the need for accessibility.

9.1 What You Need to Know About Standards and Integration

If you need to register students, monitor their progress, and, if applicable, save test scores, you need to save the information on a Web server, and on the server you need an application that can identify the learner information. The server side is where learning management systems (LMSs) and collection engines work.

From a practical point of view, every software developer has its own idea of what information needs to be saved and stored, the name of the field in which the information is to be saved, and the format in which it is to be saved. This is fine if the developer has created an end-to-end solution. Realistically, however, most organizations need a kit of tools, and integration becomes important when you want to use more then one application from more than one software developer. Integration is very expensive and very tricky without a set of standards that each developer can use when building its portion of the application so that it talks to the other applications.

AICC, SCORM, and IMS are standards that were created to ensure integration in e-learning. (IMS is a global standards organization, whose recommendations SCORM implements; IMS is not discussed separately from AICC and SCORM.) Depending on your background and responsibility, you need to know different information about these standards. For example:

- LMS and tool developers need to understand the technical details of the specification so that they can program the standards into their applications and work with other vendors to provide a complete solution.

- Course developers and training organizations need to have a basic understanding of AICC, SCORM, and IMS capabilities so that they can ask intelligent questions of their LMS and authoring tool vendors to ensure that the important information is being tracked and that their courses integrate easily with the systems.

9.2 Aviation Industry Computer-Based Training Committee (AICC): A Practical Definition

The Aviation Industry Computer-Based Training Committee (AICC) was started in the late 1980s by a group of aviation companies that needed to define a standard so that their courses would work with their LMSs. The AICC standard is broken into two major sections:

1. Course Server Communication
2. Course Structure Definition

Course Server Communication

This section defines how student results get stored and how the course player obtains user preferences; that is, it defines the communication between a course and an LMS. Specifically, it:

- Identifies how, after a student hits the complete button on a test, the test results are saved and transmitted to the server.

- Defines how the course can retrieve information, such as the student name or previous test results, from the server.

Course Structure Definition

This section defines how the server loads and broadcasts content and what content is served next. Specifically, it identifies for the LMS the start page of the course and how many Assignable Units (AU, commonly referred to as a unit) are in the course.

The AICC spec is very vague about what qualifies as a unit, providing no real definition for the term "unit" and allowing course creators to define their own definition. Before defining a unit, however, a course creator needs to understand that, from the LMS's point of view, a unit is the next element that the LMS serves. The most popular definition for a unit has turned out to be a page, but it can also be defined as any element, including a chapter or a course.

- The benefit of defining a unit as a chapter is that a student can navigate an entire chapter without having to wait for the LMS to serve each page.
- If the course is defined as a unit, the learner can roam around an entire course without having to wait for the LMS to serve each page. This definition is useful when you are creating courses as a reusable reference material.

The loophole, so to speak, in AICC is that implementing the LMS's specifications is not required, only recommended; that is, the authoring tool and the LMS vendor can opt to implement a feature—or not—and there is even leeway in how the feature may be implemented. As a result, most authoring tools and LMSs take the easiest way out. They implement the fewest features needed to pass the self test. Typically, that amounts to the ability to send and store start of course and end of course. Some authoring tools and LMSs don't even send and store grades. A minimal LMS considers a learner's course complete when "end of course" is sent.

With a minimum implementation, lots of would-be beneficial information is lost. For example, suppose an employee takes a compliance course on the company's alcohol policy and passes the test with a score of 80 percent. Then the employee is caught violating the policy. If you stored a grade and saved all the answers to the test questions, you have proof that the employee was aware of the policy and understood the rules. Without the detail, all you know is that the employee took the course.

9.3 Sharable Content Object Reference Model (SCORM): A Practical Definition

Sharable Content Object Reference Model (SCORM) is an initiative started by the U.S. government's secretary of defense.

Advanced Distributed Learning (ADL) Co-Labs actually developed the SCORM standard. SCORM became the dominant standard when the U.S. government mandated that all federal organizations must use SCORM. AICC and IMS standards have now become subsets of SCORM because the SCORM standard is made up of standards created by the AICC and LMS committees.

SCORM V 1.2

Every few years, SCORM releases a new version of its standards. Currently, the most widely adopted SCORM standard is V 1.2.

- This version picks up from the AICC definitions discussed earlier and cleans up some of AICC's problems.
- The SCORM course structure component contains the same information as the AICC component, but in a more flexible format.
- The course-to-LMS communication specification is likewise based on the AICC specification, but it is more clearly defined and better architected so that it works more effectively with modern browsers.

The 1.2 specification has a couple of downsides:

- A lot of data that the course could transmit to the LMS is still marked optional. Consequently, most LMSs have not chosen to support these fields, and this decision limits the amount of learner information that can be gathered and saved. For example, most LMSs still don't save learner answers to specific questions.
- Only linear sequencing of a course is supported; that is, learners cannot randomly access information; they can only go to the next unit.

SCORM 2004

SCORM 2004 is the latest implementation. It:

- Cleans up some of the definitions found in SCORM 1.2.
- Requires LMSs to support more data.
- Allows components to be shared between units.
- Includes support for sequencing and navigation.

This means that the SCORM 2004 version supports more usable data storage by requiring LMSs to store more fields. The biggest improvement is that an LMS must now store student answers if the course reports them. In SCORM 1.2, the course developer had to declare, in the course structure file, every piece of content that would be used by each unit. With SCORM 2004, components of a course can be shared between units. The benefit is that a course developer can identify components that are shared between units. An example of a shared component is a glossary. In SCORM 2004, a glossary of terms can be accessed by any unit in a course without having to be a part of the unit.

The biggest change in SCORM 2004 is the ability to have sequencing and navigation. This allows for complex logic identifying which unit should be served next to students, based on their performance. It also allows for the creation of scores based on combinations of submodule scores; that is, each learner can be served a different series of pages based on their answers to a series of questions.

This advanced logic sounds very compelling from a high-level point of view, but it becomes a nightmare in implementation. The intelligence of the logic quickly becomes complicated and cannot be easily simplified. When course flow and logic are very complex, the course comes to be database driven. Due to the level of sophistication needed to develop these types of courses, developers, SMEs, and trainers become excluded from much of the course creation process. Courses with these advanced logic capabilities need to be designed by very experienced, high-level, database and data mining experts.

Organizations need to look at the time and cost of course development to identify whether they have the budget to develop a course with these capabilities. The fully burdened cost of a database-driven system with these advanced performance capabilities (hardware, software, and the people to run it) is upward of $1,750,000 (estimated at hardware = $250,000; software = $500,000; people/service = $1,000,000), and individual courses may cost upward of $150,000 each to develop.

9.4 Sharable Content Object (SCO)

Many discussions concerning SCORM center on SCOs. A SCORM SCO (Sharable Content Object) is what AICC calls a unit or Assignable Unit. Either an SCO or a unit is the same thing: an element that is assigned and tracked. It can be a test question, a picture, a page, a chapter, or a course.

Unfortunately, many LMSs and authoring tools have a very limited reading and implantation of SCOs, thereby limiting what course creators can do. Specifically, many developers have decided that an SCO must be a single page of content. With that definition, course creators are forced to chunk their content down to a page, creating a terrible experience for learners because it forces them to go from SCO to SCO when they move from page to page. In addition, when an LMS handles delivery, it can slow down the experience because, every time a page is requested, the LMS needs to close the current page and launch the next one (as opposed to having a Web server display the next page). With some LMSs, when requesting the next SCO, the user must return to the table of contents and then choose the next page from a listing of available SCOs. Another big problem with defining a SCO as a page is LMS response time. Most LMSs, when closing one SCO and launching the next, have a delay time, which can be as long as 20 seconds when going from unit to unit—even on a good DSL line.

SCO Definitions and Design Limitations

One reason many LMSs define the SCO as a page is to get around their design limitations:

- Most LMSs don't capture or report interactions and objectives. So the only way they can have granularity of reporting is to force granularity of content.

- Using SCOs to make up for insufficient design is also done in testing. Many LMSs that are unable to save test question responses have gotten around this limitation by making each test question an SCO. Technically, implementing a single question on a Web page is easy, but instructionally it is a frustrating for the learner.

- Another tragedy of poor LMS design is that it becomes impossible to use the LMS to carry out surveys and assessments. The benefit of designing an SCO to be more than a single page is that you can include a summary as part of it, providing your courses with navigation and reusability without making compromises.

The upshot is that course creators should identify at what level they want to make content SCOs based on their learning objectives and learners' experience, not on their LMSs weaknesses.

The good news is that some LMSs do capture and report interactions and objectives and do not limit SCOs to a page: Avilar, Oracle, MeridianKSI, IBM, and Aspen. So there is hope that your LMS can be used to evaluate whether the instructor is giving bad questions and to get insight into your learner's thoughts. If you want to see a tool that uses chapters or entire courses as a SCO, look at the ReadyGo Web Course Builder.

9.5 Sharable and Reusable Content

Sharable and reusable content is another popular conversation in SCORM circles. There are four approaches to maximizing reuse of content:

1. Redeployment of existing courses.

2. The ability to rearrange existing units to create new courses (most commonly referred to as sharable content).

3. The support of learners to revisit content as just-in-time learning.

4. The ability to convert content for use in other scenarios, such as mobile, PowerPoint, or a user manual.

The objectives of sharing and reusing content are to save money and to maximize use of already created materials. Unfortunately, most people have narrowed their definition to include only the second objective, rearranging pieces to create new courses. This narrow definition is far too limiting.

Current e-learning wisdom says that the smaller the grain of content is, the more places it can be used. However, the reality is that the smaller the grain of content is, the less relevance the grain has with other grains. For example, a picture might be used on a page to visually support a point, but the same picture on a different page may be irrelevant or confusing.

Information Access Versus Course Creation

The broad definition of reusable content being bandied about to-day claims that the goal is to let the learner take resources from several courses and to have the server put them together at delivery time to create a new course. This definition is probably unworkable because it creates courses that look like ransom notes. When large corporations look into these systems, their real goal seems to be to create transparency and accessibility so that corporate information is easily available to all employees. My response is that e-learning is not the solution for all content issues. If your goal is to provide access to corporate information, then create a corporate repository, and use content management tools, not e-learning tools. Training serves a different purpose from information access. Organizations would be much better served if they defined e-learning reusability as the ability to move courses from LMS to LMS with the course behaving the same and if they viewed content reusability as a different requirement.

LMS Compatibility

The SCORM standard focuses on providing a framework that permits courses to be moved from one LMS to another. LMS vendors have interpreted this plug-and-play standard as the ability to redeliver learning objects in a new course by having a database reassemble the content. However, this interpretation is self serving. It is in an LMS's best interest not to support plug-in-play courses, but rather to sell expensive and complicated solutions. Thus LMSs interpret sharability and reusability to include a complicated database with expensive support services to get the database working.

Training or content managers who have a large quantity of existing courses and presentations find this LMS argument compelling. Creating courses, documentation, workbooks, and brochures is time-consuming and expensive. Being able to identify, find, and repurpose content has always been the holy grail of anyone in content management.

The issue is that, from a proactive, course development point of view, you need to be intimately familiar with content before you can reuse it because your course needs to tell a cohesive story. In many of these database-driven systems, granularity turns into a problem because the LMSs define a learning object as a page or a single test question. This definition is too small to create functioning training. Chapters are a better level of granularity because each page has the same context as the next page. Chapter granularity makes e-learning an effective reference material because a learner can use a key word search and then land on a page with the key word or statistics they are looking for. Using the search tool or built-in chapter navigation to find a page creates a useful and reusable object, whereas a page or a test question on its own is not necessary useful.

The Fallacy of All-Purpose LMSs

When organizations clearly define their content goals up front and then identify the right solution to store and access the solutions, they save money and arrive at better solutions for the corporate content issues. An effective approach along these lines is to identify which of three categories the content falls into:

1. *Informational:* This kind of content—information that stands on its own—should be served from a wiki.

2. *Archived:* Content that has been produced and needs to be available to the organization, such as all those thousands of PowerPoint presentations or Word documents, should be electronically archived on a corporate document management system.

3. *Learning:* When content is in a format for learning (includes instructional design) and is used to explain a new or difficult subject, it should be placed on an LMS.

Despite these clearly distinct types of content, many LMSs want to sell their solution so that they are all things to all people. However, most solutions that reach too far provide a weak solution for everyone. You need more than one solution to solve content management access. The lesson is to stay away from solutions that purport to create full training courses from individual pages of content.

On the training side, what typically works best for organizations that want to reuse training modules is a repository of existing courses. For large organizations, learning modules (units or SCOs) like chapters, glossaries, and pictures can be annotated and saved in a database so that other trainers can reuse them. Smaller organizations can create a simple system for saving individual chapters and glossaries by placing them all on a shared server with an easy-to-identify labeling system.

Regardless of your solution, just make sure your authoring tool supports chapters as units or SCOs. Your course creators can then reassemble, update, and edit the chapters so that they can be reused in a new course.

9.6 The Behavior of e-Learning Courses

Course behavior is what a course does with respect to the student's actions; that is, when the student does something, how does the course respond? The AICC, SCORM, and IMS specifications allow for many course content responses based on how the course author wants to deliver the content. These behaviors need to be understood before implementation because an LMS might not be able to deliver the preferred behavior. Most LMSs are designed with a specific set of behaviors, as imagined by the LMS designers. Also, the course content may produce behaviors between the course and the LMS beyond those anticipated by the LMS.

Selecting an LMS and Authoring Tool

Before selecting an LMS and authoring tools, you need to identify up front what you want the learners' experience to be. Then you need to make sure your LMS and tool can create the chosen experience. Most people have no idea what behaviors they should be looking for until it is too late. To help you identify the behaviors you need to consider when selecting a course authoring tool and an LMS, review the following list and check off the behaviors that are important to you:

___ Do you want to allow students to retake tests? Do students only have one chance to take a test, or will you allow them multiple tries? This ability affects the results that may appear in reports produced by the LMS.

___ If you allow students to take the test more then once, do you want the previous results overwritten? If you allow students to retake tests, do you want to see how many times they took it and their scores for each time? Most LMSs overwrite previous answers if you allow students to take a test more than once.

___ Can students come back to the content that they have completed? This capability is desirable if you want to make class material available as reference material. However, many LMSs either don't support it or change the student's status when they revisit a course. This leads to misleading reports.

___ Do you want learners to be able to look through the material when taking a test? You may want the session to be accessible after they have taken the course, but you do not want them to be able to review material when taking the test.

___ How do you declare content "complete" (a SCORM specification)? LMSs arbitrarily designate the definition of "complete."

___ Is completion based on a student's having read all the content or on the learner's passing specific tests?

___ Does the LMS shut or close the browser when the student exits the unit or SCO? The SCORM specification implies that the LMS is responsible for opening and closing browser windows (not the course), but many LMSs leave this as responsibility of the course content.

___ How do you define where the learner is in the course? The SCORM specification has a field called "lesson_location," which can be used to define the current page or progress through the course. Which do you want? What does your LMS support?

___ How do you want to define the field in SCORM called "score"? LMSs define it variously. Some use the score variable for test grade, and others use it for progress.

___ What happens if you have multiple tests in one unit or SCO? Do the scores from the various tests get individually saved, or are they averaged? What happens if the student takes the various tests in separate sessions?

___ How does your LMS store and report results? Are reports available? What specifically do they save?

Having made these choices, make sure your solutions can respond appropriately before making purchases. Each of the LMS and authoring tool vendors has made different assumptions when creating their application. You need to know what assumptions they have made so that you understand how they save information. You then need to map how these tools work to what you want. If they don't map, you can either modify what you want or choose a different tool so that your courses save information and respond the way you want them to. Some LMS applications are more flexible then others. Price and marketing have absolutely nothing to do with the quantity, quality, and flexibility of a tool or LMS to send and save information.

9.7 Questions to Ask

To get the solution that works for your organization, you must ask the right questions of the vendor. A good start is to go through the questions on desired behaviors in the preceding list, that is, identify what experience you want your learners to have and identify what information you want to save.

The most basic questions that managers and course developers need to ask of their LMS and tool vendors are:

- What standards do you support?
- How much of the standard have you implemented?

Specifically, go through your answers to the behavior questions and see whether the authoring tool can send the information and whether the LMS can receive it. Getting a support person from a large authoring tool company like Microsoft or Adobe to answer your questions can be difficult, because they are not very responsive and often tell you that your problem is a known bug or that you need to upgrade to the most recent version before they can answer your question. Microsoft does not support SCORM. Adobe only minimally supports it; that is, Adobe sends a start, stop, and, if applicable, one grade per unit. A unit can be one quiz question developed in a graphic tool like Adobe's Captivate.

If you decide that the intended behaviors require more than minimal support, you need to layer your authoring tools, that is, create a page in Dreamweaver and then use a tool like ReadyGo WCB as a container. Dreamweaver provides no SCORM support. However, ReadyGo WCB provides a very high level of SCORM support and becomes a container, allowing Microsoft, Dreamweaver, or Captivate pages to work within its pages. ReadyGo can then perform all the SCORM communication.

Also ask your authoring tool company whether it has customized its implementation for different LMSs. Each LMS implements the standards slightly differently; a course saved as SCORM might not work with any "SCORM" LMS. Most authoring tools have successfully run a sample course through ADL/SCORM self-test, but this tests only the minimum capabilities.

You need to take responsibility for your solution. Ask your authoring tool vendor whether it has a specific implementation for the LMS you have or are planning on getting. If they say yes, then:

- Ask the authoring tool vendor to provide you with the fields they support.
- Ask your LMS what fields they support.
- Map the two sets of fields.

If the authoring tool sends only a subset of the required information to the LMS, your course will not do what you want it to do. This step might sound painful, but it is worth taking. You do not need to know too much about the fields. You just need to map name to name. If you skip this step and your LMS can't save what you want or your authoring tool can't send what you need, you will be spending a lot of time and money for a solution that does not work.

9.8 The Meaning of Accessibility

A separate and different issue from SCORM is accessibility, which is all about making Web pages available to people with disabilities. Probably the most prevalent populations requiring broad technical adaptations to provide them with Web access are those who are blind and deaf.

In the United States, accessibility for persons with visual, hearing, and other impairments is covered under the Americans with Disabilities Act (ADA) and Section 508 of the Assistive Technology Act of 1998. The European Union (EU) and Canadian federal government also require accessibility, and they follow the W3C accessibility guidelines, which provide more detail and have stiffer requirements than the ADA and Section 508. Any federal organization, any organization that hires blind or deaf employees, or any organization that provides training to the general marketplace are subject accessibility requirements.

Also remember that many members of the aging workforce and senior citizens may have vision and hearing impairments. If your organization serves senior citizens and you want your courses to be accessible to them, you should make sure that your courses and learning infrastructure meet accessibility guidelines.

Persons who are blind obviously have different requirements than those who are deaf. Most Web pages are accessible to the deaf—unless you have decided to create courses that are, say, voice-annotated PowerPoint presentations (as discussed, a poor solution for e-learning in any case). Obviously, voice-annotated PowerPoint is completely inaccessible to the deaf learner, but not so obviously, it can also be a frustrating experience for the blind learner. Whereas the average sighted person receives only 10 percent from auditory sources, blind people receive 60 to 70 percent of their cues from auditory sources. Most blind people play their screen readers up to three or more times faster than we speak. As a result, a voice-over might appear to make your slide show more accessible, but it makes for a frustrating experience when it is playing in competition with a text-to-speech screen reader.

Ensuring That Your Tools Meet Accessibility Requirements

A lot of tools out there are supposed to be ADA/508 compliant for screen readers, but, due to the stiffer W3C requirements, few claim to be W3C compliant. If your goal is to create accessible courses, you should see a huge red flag if you find a tool that claims Section 508 compliance but not W3C compliance. There is no true standard or set of requirements for functional accessibility under Section 508, but several levels of rigid standards and requirements have to be met to claim W3C compliance. Many LMS and authoring tools take advantage of the low barrier in the United States to claim ADA/508 compliance. They do little, however, to make their courses really usable by people accessing content with screen reading adaptations, all the while claiming that they meet the standards.

Many organizations do not test to see whether their courses are actually accessible; they just take the vendor's word and assume their courses are accessible. For example:

- Anything produced in Flash is not accessible unless a programmer has read Adobe's accessibility guidelines and modified the Flash module. This module, built into Flash, has not been programmed for accessibility and has menu options that provide the sighted student with visual clues and a detailed menu, but the blind student can hear only "Button 1," "Button 2," "Button 3." This shortcoming leaves the blind learner without any ability to decipher what the menus mean.

- Courses built with WYSIWYG tools that visually lay out a page typically save text as a graphic. As a graphic, that text is completely inaccessible to the blind student's screen reader. On some WYSIWYG tools, you can turn on an ADA/508 feature, which includes a transparent notification that is often perceptible only with screen reading software. When accessed by the user, the learner is then taken to text at the bottom of the page or in a separate file, providing either less information than what the sighted student receives or information out of context. The effect is a long page of text that often lacks continuity and that is not easily navigable in the context of the course.

- Many courses use features like "Click here" icons to turn a page, and these are functionally inaccessible to a blind student who can't see where "here" is.

If your goal is simply to say you are ADA/508 compliant, then none of this matters. If your goal is to allow blind and deaf people functional access to your courses, then you need to make sure your tool really does create functionally accessible content.

• • • • • • • • • • • •

Case Study: Blair & Associates

Roger Blair, an accessible and assistive technology computer support specialist, conducts adaptive computer training for public and private sector customers with disabilities as an offering of his consultancy, Blair & Associates. Blair, himself blind from birth, comments that for blind people, accessibility is all about access to content and ease of course navigation with a keyboard. He likes to say that it is not really hard to create functional accessibility; authors just need to keep it clean and simple. Roger states that screen layout can create havoc; many visually complex screens can be difficult to navigate with a screen reader because the software can track only from left to right and from top to bottom. He has found that LMSs like Moodle and Blackboard, although Section 508 compliant, incorporate far too many inaccessible synchronous tools surrounding course content, severely disrupting the learning process for students accessing coursework with screen readers.

The problem is that the solutions are too frequently created by fully sighted developers who have never experienced access through assistive technologies in their day-to-day lives. These developers might make sure links use real words that can be accessible to screen readers, but they then lay out their information with a completely daunting interface. Most of these interfaces are so overwhelming or mouse dependent that a blind student cannot navigate through them efficiently, if at all. On the administrative side of course creation, Roger has found the interfaces to be completely nonnavigable and inaccessible to screen readers.

When accessing a course, Roger finds that the best of them allow him to directly land on headings or blocks of text using minimal keystrokes. Visual readers can scan an unfamiliar page and quickly focus on relevant headings and main text. The blind student, visiting the same page for the first time, needs to read every element on it to understand the structure of the page. On pages that are laid out poorly, he spends a lot of time navigating each text block, line by line, so that he can make sure he is not missing information.

. . . .

Tools like ReadyGo WCB that truly adhere to ADA and W3C compliance include simple capabilities like enabled access keys that enable a learner to land on a page.

Learners can press alt and a preassigned access letter on the keyboard and be taken to each page element or related block of text. They do not need to navigate each block on the page to ascertain the page layout. They can also use similar functions, such as alt+p[revious] or alt+n[ext], to move back and forth from page to page.

Screen Readers

If you do not use a screen reader, how do you know that your courses are accessible? Ask your vendor the following questions. If they don't answer yes, then you know your courses will not be functionally accessible to blind students using screen readers.

- When a page loads, can the screen reader skip all the table navigation and go directly to the title, then to the main content text block?
- Can the learner use access keys to navigate page elements and move efficiently from block to block and from page to

page? (Try navigating your own course by keyboard without the aid of the mouse.)

- Are there provisions for all graphics to have appropriate alt tags? (Can a screen reader provide a legible description of the graphic?)

- Do active buttons and other interactive page elements contain informational text labels? (Be sure to incorporate associated hyperlinks to graphical page elements for ease of keyboard navigation and access.)

- Can low-vision students adjust text size and color contrast in course pages to meet their visual requirements?

9.9 Checklist

___ There are four approaches to maximizing reuse of content. Which approach are you attempting to achieve?

1. Redeployment of existing courses:
2. Ability to rearrange existing units to create new courses (commonly referred to as sharable content).
3. Support of learners to revisit content as just-in-time learning.
4. Ability to convert content for use in other scenario, such as mobile, PPT, or a user manual.

___ The most basic questions you need to ask an LMS and tool vendor are:

1. What standards do you support?
2. How much of the standard have you implemented?

___ What behaviors do you want in your courses?

1. Do you want to allow students to retake tests? Do students only have one chance to take a test, or will you allow them multiple tries? This ability affects the results that may appear in reports produced by the LMS.

2. If you allow students to take the test more then once, do you want the previous results overwritten? If you allow students to retake tests, do you want to see how many times they took it and their scores for each time? Most LMSs overwrite previous answers if you allow students to take a test more than once.

3. Can students come back to the content that they have completed? This capability is desirable if you want to make class material available as reference material. However, many LMSs either don't support it or change the student's status when they revisit a course. This leads to misleading reports.

4. Do you want learners to be able to look through the material when taking a test? You may want the session to be accessible after they have taken the course, but you do not want them to be able to review material when taking the test.

5. How do you declare content "complete" (a SCORM specification)? LMSs arbitrarily designate the definition of "complete."

6. Is completion based on a student's having read all the content or on the learner's passing specific tests?

7. Does the LMS shut or close the browser when the student exits the unit or SCO? The SCORM specification implies that the LMS is responsible for opening and closing browser windows (not the course), but many LMSs leave this as responsibility of the course content.

8. How do you define where the learner is in the course? The SCORM specification has a field called "lesson_ location," which can be used to define the current page or progress through the course. Which do you want? What does your LMS support?

9. How do you want to define the field in SCORM called "score"? LMSs define it variously. Some use the score variable for test grades, and others use it for progress.

10. What happens if you have multiple tests in one unit or SCO? Do the scores from the various tests get individually saved, or are they averaged? What happens if the student takes the various tests in separate sessions?
11. How does your LMS store and report results? Are reports available? What specifically do they save?

__ Questions to ask to assure course accessibility:

1. When a page loads, can the screen reader skip all the table navigation and go directly to the title, then to the main content text block?
2. Ca the learner use access keys to navigate page elements and move efficiently from block to block and from page to page? (Try navigating your own course by keyboard without the aid of the mouse.)
3. Are there provisions for all graphics to have appropriate alt tags? (Can a screen reader provide a legible description of the graphic?)
4. Do active buttons and other interactive page elements contain informational text labels? (Be sure to incorporate associated hyperlinks to graphical page elements for ease of keyboard navigation and access.)
5. Can low-vision students adjust text size and color contrast in course pages to meet their visual requirements?

10.0

Conclusion: LMS/Tools with Good Implementation

Evaluations of implementations are subjective. You need to know what you want to do and then be assured your vendor of choice can meet the needs. Before choosing a vendor have a clear idea of:

- What you want to create.
- What information you want to save.
- What experience you want your learner to have.

Once you choose a vendor, you should not have to think about standards. If the vendors have truly met the requirements, standards should be trivial matters for the course creator and invisible to the learners.

In the beginning of the book, I stated that, to achieve the best results with e-learning, you need to identify an optimal learner experience and the information you want to save. Throughout this book, my goals have been to:

- Explain the pros and cons of different trends and technologies.
- Identify possible learner experiences.
- Outline what I have found that works well.
- Provide guidelines for identifying your optimal experience.

Specifically, in Chapter 1.0, I recommended identifying clear goals that are measurable and actionable and described how to identify your learner audience. Creating such goals and identifying the specific audience provide you with a document that facilitates effective communication within the organization and successfully frames your e-learning initiative.

In Chapter 2.0 we discussed the stages that organizations go through when integrating a new technology or initiative into how they do business. I hope this gave you insight into where your organization is so that you can more effectively move it to a more productive position in the future. I also outlined the basics of creating effective Web content.

In Chapter 3.0 I outlined the different types of e-learning. Organizations that learn how to quickly assess the appropriate approach to creating a course save time and money in the long run.

In Chapters 4.0 and 5.0 I explained the trends and technologies of Web 2.0.

In Chapter 6.0 I defined which of these trends and technologies are applicable to e-learning and the best-use practices when deploying e-learning 2.0.

In Chapter 7.0 I moved from the theoretical to the practical by outlining guidelines for creating effective rapid e-learning courses. Specifically:

- Length of course.
- How to flesh out an outline or PowerPoint presentation so that it can stand on its own.
- Strategies for creating a more active experience by creating drill-downs and testing.

In Chapter 8.0 I discussed when and where to use graphics, audio, Flash, and video, so that you can create a more effective experience.

Finally, in Chapter 9.0, I explained SCORM, AICC, and the practices most closely associated with these technologies. Where applicable, I have provided you with checklists that you can use in your e-learning initiative.

My hope is that this book has provided you with enough effective insight into e-learning that you can more effectively focus an existing initiatives or create effective guidelines for new ones.

I am on-line at anitarosen.com and am always interested in hearing from my readers at anita@readygo.com.

Resources

Anyone who is truly interested in producing functionally accessible courses should visit Jim Thatcher's Web site: jimthatcher.com. Jim, an accessibility expert, has created an excellent, easy-to-follow tutorial highlighting how to create truly accessible Web pages.

Another excellent source of information and evaluation tools that you can use yourself to determine the functional accessibility of your e-learning tools is the Consortium for E-learning Accessibility/C4EA, home of e-Learn-ViP (e-learning for visually impaired persons). Tools can be downloaded from http://www.e-learn-vip.org.

See a CSS demonstration. See the same page with different looks http://www.csszengarden.com. Examples from Zen Garden were given earlier in this book, in chapter 2 Figure 2.2a and Figure 2.2b. These illustrations are screen snapshots from Zen Garden showing the exact same content displayed very differently.

Appendix

Author Guide

This is a guide that subject matter experts (SMEs) can use to plan their courses. The recommendations in this guide assist SMEs to create instructionally sound content that easily flows into an e-learning authoring tool.

Guidelines for Creating an Effective Web Course

Divide the course information into small chunks. Students typically have a 15- to 20-minute attention span when taking Web courses. Use the following guidelines when dividing the course into small sections (see Figure A.1):

- Create five or fewer chapters per course. If you have more then six chapters, consider breaking the content into multiple courses.
- Each chapter should consist of about 10 to 15 pages. Avoid having more then 20 pages in a chapter.

Figure A.1 Course organization.

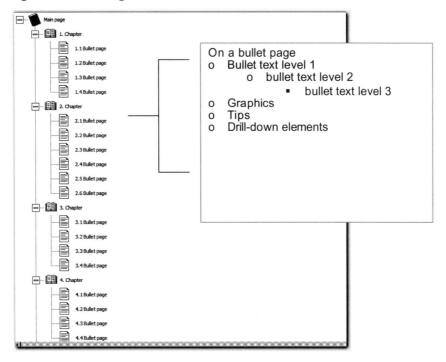

- Limit the number of bulleted points on each page. Your goal should be a maximum of five bullets per page, with no more than three levels of indentation.

- Keep questions to about 10 to 15 per chapter.

- If applicable, create a glossary of between 10 and 15 words. Each word should have a description of one or two sentences.

- Summaries help to frame the material to be presented. Throughout the course there are many places to add a summary.

Using Learning Objectives

To create a better focused course that will meet business objectives it is recommend that you start out by creating a list of learning objectives for the course. For example, "By the end of this course you will be able to. . . ."

- For your course learning objectives, list three to five goals or learning objectives.
- Include these learning objectives or goals in your course summary.
  - Make sure that your course content covers these goals.
  - If the content does not cover your course goals, create additional chapters or pages to your existing presentation.
- For each chapter, create three to five goals or learning objectives.
  - Use these learning objectives or goals in your chapter summary.
  - Review the pages in your PowerPoint presentation to make sure they meet your learning objectives.
  - If your content does not meet your learning objectives, create additional pages to your existing presentation.

Main Page

Every course should have a main introduction page, similar to a book's cover, that contains the following (see Figure A.2):

1. A title.

2. One or two sentences that describe the course and provide a course objective such as, "When you complete this course, you will be proficient in. . . ."

3. An optional graphic that would work well on the main page of the course.

Figure A.2 Sample of a main introduction page.

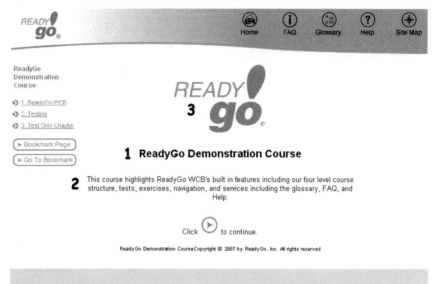

Chapter Title Pages

Each chapter should have a title page that contains the following (see Figure A.3):

1. *A short title:* If you have chosen to create a course chapter listing on a sidebar, choose a short title that fits nicely in your sidebar. For example, the full chapter title may be "The Introduction of Printing Machines in the Twentieth Century," but the short title could be something shorter, such as "Printing Machines."

2. *A chapter title:* You can write a long and expressive chapter title to be displayed on the chapter title page.

3. *A chapter summary:* This highlights the goals and learning objectives of the chapter. Keep this under four sentences.

4. *The index:* This is automatically created from your page titles when you generate your course. To make your

Figure A.3 Sample chapter title page.

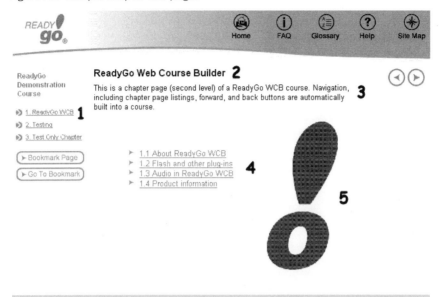

chapter and index an effective resource, consider varying the page titles.

5. *Chapter picture:* You may optionally include a graphic to be displayed on the chapter title page.

Bullet Pages

Bullet pages provide the core course content. Bullet pages consist of the following elements:

1. *Title:* Make the title unique so that it provides effective navigation.
2. This frames the ideas to be presented on that page.
3. *Bulleted points:* The course content should be provided in bulleted points. (See Figure A.4.)

Figure A.4 Sample bullet page.

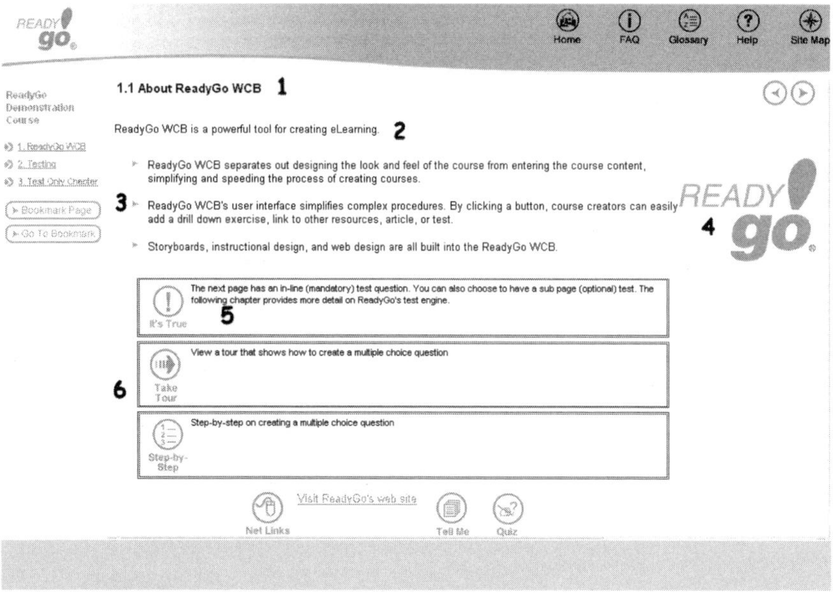

- You may need additional refinement of your bullet points. If you need too many levels, consider breaking your subject into multiple pages.
- Studies have found that students have between 48 and 120 percent higher retention levels when they receive information in bulleted points over paragraphs.
- It is best to have bullets with three or less levels of indentation.

4. *Graphics:* You may have multiple graphics on a page.
5. *Tip or It's true:* Use to highlight an interesting fact.
6. *A drill-down element:* Use to provide supportive information by letting the learner drill down to receive additional information. Don't just tell the learner; show the learner. One way is to identify the sources you used to create your course. Do you know a good Web site that has pertinent information? Give the link. Provide the exact URL and

the text you want them to see. Drill-down elements consist of:

- ○ *Exercises or tours:* These may include optional videos and exercises.
- ○ *Step-by-step instructions:* Information broken down and laid out in a series of steps, which can include graphics.
- ○ *Articles:* Text or PDF articles can be included.
- ○ *Links to external Web sites:* No more than five per page.

Tests

Use test questions to ensure that the student understands the material and is not flipping through the course.

1. *Tests within a chapter:* Use test questions within a chapter to make the material interactive.
   - ○ *Get the student thinking about the material:* Ask a question before presenting a new subject. If they are taking a course on e-learning, you might ask them, "Have you ever taken a course on e-learning? Answer Yes or No." This gets them thinking about the subject you are about to present.
   - ○ *Remember the most important point you just taught them:* Ask them a question that highlights the most important point. This makes sure they read the material and that it helps highlight the point.
2. *End-of-chapter tests:* At the end of the chapter, you should create a 5- to 10-question test to ensure that the learners have read and remember the points you brought up in the chapter. You can use the same test questions used throughout the chapter. Repetition helps students remember important points.
3. *End-of-course test:* Use the end-of-course test to ensure that the student has learned the material you presented. You can use test questions from the chapters.

Glossary

The glossary consists of (see Figure A.5):

1. *The term:* A word to be defined.
2. *A definition:* One to three sentences defining the term.
3. *Options* such as:
   ○ A graphic that helps explain the word.
   ○ A link to a resource, such as Wikipedia.

Figure A.5 Sample glossary.

Sample Course Content

Here is an example of the material developed for a course:

Course Title	ReadyGo Demonstration Course.
Course Summary	This course highlights ReadyGo WCB's built in features, including our four-level course structure, tests, exercises, navigation, and services including the glossary, FAQ, and Help.
Chapter 1 Title	ReadyGo Web Course Builder.
Chapter 1 Sidebar Title	ReadyGo WCB.

Chapter 1 Summary	This is a chapter page (second level) of a ReadyGo WCB course. Navigation, including chapter page listings. Forward and back buttons are automatically built into a course.
Chapter 1, Page 1 **Page Title** **Page Summary**	About ReadyGo WCB. ReadyGo WCB is a powerful tool for creating e-learning.
Bullet Points	<ul><li>ReadyGo WCB separates designing the look and feel of the course from entering the course content, simplifying and speeding the process of creating courses.</li><li>ReadyGo WCB's user interface simplifies complex procedures. By clicking a button, course creators can easily add a drill-down exercise or link to other resources, an article, or a test.</li><li>Storyboards, instructional design, and Web design are all built into the ReadyGo WCB.</li></ul>
It's True!	The next page has an in-line (mandatory) test question. You can also choose to have a subpage (optional) test. The following chapter provides more detail on ReadyGo's test engine.
Net Link	Visit ReadyGo's Web site $\longrightarrow$ http://www.readygo.com.
Drill-Down Article **Drill-Down Title** **Drill-Down Content**	Tell Me More. A Tell Me More page provides a mechanism to provide expanded

details on a subject. The bullet page is typically used to provide the overview of the subject, but learners usually need more detail to achieve an in-depth understanding of the subject. Tell Me More articles can be as long as the author wants. However, it is best to keep articles to a few paragraphs for learners who read from their computer screen. This article includes text and an Adobe PDF file.

Test

Question 1   The Summer 2008 Olympics will be held in:

Question Type   Multiple Choice
Answers

A. Sydney
Feedback if selected: The 2000 Olympics were held in Sydney. The 2008 Olympics will be held in Beijing.

B. Beijing
Feedback if selected: Yes, the 2008 Olympics will be held in Beijing.

C. Athens
Feedback if selected: The 2004 Olympics were held in Athens. The 2008 Olympics will be held in Beijing.

D. London
Feedback if selected: The 2012 Olympics will be held in London. The 2008 Olympics will be held in Beijing.

Right Answer	B.
Question 2	A cross-country foot race of 26 miles, 385 yards is called a:
Question Type	Text Entry
	Feedback if correct: Yes, a 26-mile cross-country foot race is called a marathon.
	Feedback if wrong: A 26-mile cross-country foot race is called a marathon.
Right Answer	Marathon.
Question 3	Within 0.5 seconds, what is the World Record for the men's 100-meter race?
Question Type	Numeric.
	Feedback if correct: Correct, the men's 100-meter race is run in less than 10 seconds.
	Feedback if wrong: The world record for the men's 100-meter sprint is about 9.7 seconds.
Right Answer	9.200000–10.300000.
Question 4	Do you agree or disagree? The Olympics should be held only in Greece.
Question Type	Preference; not graded
	A. Strongly Disagree.
	B. Strongly Agree.
	C. No Opinion.

Glossary

Application service Service that is accessible over the Web, without the user having to download any new software.

Application service provider (ASP) or hosted solution Company that provides applications that are accessible over the Web.

Asynchronous e-learning Taking training courses on-line, at the time of your choosing, by yourself, and self-guided.

Asynchronous JavaScript and XML (AJAX) Programming language that allows a combination of the browser and server to be more flexible so that there is interactivity in a client's browser.

Aviation Industry Computer-Based Training Committee (AICC) International association of technology-based training professionals that develops standards for serving e-learning courses.

Blog Website where entries are written and displayed.

Cascading Style Sheets (CSS) Language used to describe the presentation (Web page design) of a document written in a markup language (HTML or XML).

Connecting technologies Technologies that work between the browser and server applications: Common Gateway Interface (CGI), Active Server Pages (ASP), ColdFusion, and Java 2 Enterprise Edition (J2EE).

Extensible Markup Language (XML) General-purpose markup language that allows users to define their own tags.

Forum Web application for holding discussions and posting user-generated content. Also called Web forums, message boards, discussion boards, (electronic) discussion groups, discussion forums, and bulletin boards.

Hypertext Markup Language (HTML) Markup language that most Web pages are currently being developed in.

Learning management system (LMS) Software system used to manage students and courses.

Learning content management system (LCMS) Learning management system that also supports the creation, storage, reuse, and management of courses in a central repository.

Mashup Taking two or more of anything and mixing them together to create something new. In this book mashups are sites that take content from two or more services and combines them into Web page or service.

Microcontent Small training sessions that are taken as the need arises.

New software languages Programming languages are fast to write because they are good at processing text and don't need to be compiled: Perl, PHP, and TCL (pronounced tickle).

Podcast Digital file distributed over the Internet for playback on portable media players and personal computers.

Rapid asynchronous e-learning Fast and simple method of creating an asynchronous e-learning course.

Return on investment (ROI) Percentage used to evaluate the efficiency of an investment.

Rich site summary (RSS) Broadcast tool, or digital feed, that is used to send digital content over the Internet.

Scripting languages Helper applications that take information passed to them and display it in the browser: JavaScript, VBScript, Java, and ActionScript (Flash).

Semantic Web Evolving extension of the World Wide Web in which Web content can be found, shared, and integrated more easily.

Smartphone Cell phone or PDA with a Web browser.

Subject matter expert (SME) Person who knows the material being developed.

Synchronous e-learning On-line training courses taken at the same time and through the same mechanism as other students and an instructor.

Traditional asynchronous e-learning High production method of creating asynchronous e-learning course.

Web 2.0 Description of Web services and supporting technologies being developed after 2005.

Wikipedia On-line encyclopedia using wiki guidelines.

World Wide Web Consortium (W3C) Main international standards organization for the World Wide Web.

XSL (Extensible Style Sheet Language) The display format for XML pages.

Index